FROM THE EDITOR

WHEN MY FAMILY AND I DECIDED, some ten years ago, to move into Knole, we had little idea what we were undertaking. Floorboards were lifted, walls knocked through, and layers of the house stripped back, in our attempt to adapt a corner of this Jacobean palace for 21st-century domestic living. I was, at the time, writing a book about Knole and the Sackville family who have lived here for the past 400 years. As I did so, I was – in a similar way – unpeeling centuries not just of architectural and decorative detail, but also of the private life of the house and its inhabitants.

The refurbishment of our private apartments was tiny in scale compared with the National Trust's current £20 million plan to give Knole the prominence it deserves. We had absolutely no idea of the impact of what Simon Jenkins, former Chairman of the National Trust, has described as 'the single most significant preservation and conservation project of our generation'. We couldn't imagine what it would be like to live in the middle of a building site, with a tin roof over our heads and polythene sheeting in front of the windows; or indeed what secrets would be revealed as the works progressed: the masons' marks that distinguish different periods of building, the ritualistic scratches around the fireplaces to ward off evil spirits, and the centuries of graffiti incised on the walls that tell us so much about the people who have lived and worked at Knole.

At times, the works had something of the feel of an archaeological, as much as a building site. I'm always amazed when I hear the National Trust criticised for the 'dumbing-down' of its approach, for its perceived neglect of scholarship. This has not been my experience at Knole, where every opportunity has been taken over the past few years not just to preserve the place, but also to understand it better and to interpret it more accessibly. You can see some of the fruits of that scholarly research in this edition of the Annual.

Robert Sackville-West, Lord Sackville, is the 14th generation of the Sackville family to live at Knole and the author of Inheritance: The Story of Knole and the Sackvilles (London, 2010).

COVER IMAGE
Thomas Gainsborough's *Louis-Pierre de Richebourg, marquis de Champcenetz*, 1780s, photographed at Knole, Kent
Photo: Ben Blossom, 2016

FOR THE NATIONAL TRUST
EDITOR Emma Slocombe

FOR APOLLO
APOLLO EDITOR Thomas Marks
MANAGING EDITOR Imelda Barnard
SUB-EDITORS David Gelber and Fatema Ahmed
EDITORIAL ASSISTANT Hazel Rowland
DESIGNER Will Martin

INSPIRED BY KNOLE

A £20 million project will safeguard Knole for the future, writes RICHARD HILL, while opening up new rooms to visitors and revealing much about the history of the house and its contents

UNTIL RECENTLY, KNOLE HAD NOT received the level of investment that other National Trust properties of similar significance have enjoyed in the last 70 years. The failing fabric of the building, the parlous state of the collections, and out-of-date infrastructure all meant that an ambitious plan was required to prevent Knole from deteriorating irreversibly. The house was, for instance, possibly the only great house in the Trust's care without a conservation heating system. Hence the 'Inspired by Knole' project, which was conceived in its current form in 2010 and will have cost £20m by the time of its completion in 2018. The entire scheme has always felt 'right', and has accordingly garnered support from the National Trust, the Sackville-West family, and major donors such as the Heritage Lottery Fund, the Royal Oak Foundation, and other key organisations.

On the one hand, the project is quite simple: it's about doing the right things in the right order. But on the other hand, it's an amazingly complicated undertaking, requiring many thousands of decisions, collaboration between scores of people, three-dimensional programming, and meticulous attention to detail based on thorough research. The work is of huge significance in giving this precious and precarious house and its contents a new lease of life.

Time, weather, and people had all taken their toll on both the fabric of the building and its contents. The first part of the project, which was completed in early 2014, involved making the exterior of the house wind and watertight, and protecting the area that contains the showrooms. Sun, wind, rain, snow, and dust had badly affected the external fabric – rotting the house's timber frame and external joinery, and cracking the inflexible cement render on the façades. Leadwork was failing and the glass in the windows no longer fitted properly. Structural problems were also beginning to appear. The conservation strategy has included replacing the cement with lime render (which allows the building to breathe, and is flexible so that it moves with the timber frame), careful detailing of joinery repairs, reusing the existing roof tiles wherever feasible, and using as light a touch as possible. The result, to quote Lord Sackville, has been a 'triumph'.

The next stage is the creation of the Conservation Studio and Hayloft Learning Centre in Knole's medieval barn, along with a complete refurbishment of the cafe in the Brewhouse. Recreating the original roof profile, using new Kent clay tiles capped with dressed Kentish ragstone (with its almost marble-like finish), has reunited the roofscape of Knole in a way that has not been seen since the barn roof was destroyed by fire in 1887. Inside, the contemporary finishes combined with the rough stone of the walls has created a grand space of cathedral-like proportions. It should give enormous pleasure and insight to our visitors to see the contents of Knole being preserved before their eyes.

Currently, the more painstaking work of refurbishing and redisplaying the showrooms is underway. Knole will finally have a conservation heating system (and an electrical supply that will be able to cope with more than one vacuum cleaner!). The rooms will be beautifully lit, allowing our visitors to enjoy and understand the contents in all their magnificence while maintaining the spirit of place of a house that, in the words of Lord Sackville, 'smoulders rather than sparkles'. We hope the house will look as though it has been dipped in honey.

New spaces are also being added to the visitor route, including the atmospheric and spacious Retainers Gallery in the attic and rooms that illuminate the intimate life of Eddy Sackville-West in the Gatehouse Tower. All of the work has been archaeologically surveyed and recorded, adding another layer to Knole's already rich history.

For those who have worked on the 'Inspired by Knole' project, this has been a once-in-a-lifetime experience. I hope they will treasure their contribution to the safeguarding and enrichment of this amazing house.

Richard Hill is Senior Project Manager on the 'Inspired by Knole' project.

FIG 1 The Ballroom at Knole
Photo: Cecilia Divizia, 2016

FIG 2 View from the north of Knole, which Virginia Woolf described as 'more like a town than a house'
Photo: John Miller, 2011

SOME EVIDENCE FOR 15TH-CENTURY DECORATIVE INTERIORS AT KNOLE

Knole is well known for its Jacobean decoration, but much less attention has been paid to its medieval past. As ALDEN GREGORY explains, Knole's cellar reveals a number of 15th-century wall paintings – remarkable survivals that shed new light on the architectural evolution of the house

FIG 1 Part of the scheme of wall paintings in the buttery cellar at Knole, showing a supplicant figure
Photo: Ben Blossom, 2016

WHILE KNOLE IS RENOWNED for the exceptional splendour of its Jacobean apartments, its medieval past and evidence of its medieval interiors is often overlooked. For Vita Sackville-West, writing in 1922, the medieval aspects of Knole were best viewed from the park to the north, but they presented to her a pile of grey towers, 'sombre and frowning'. The north range contained the service rooms, which were, from Vita's vantage point at least, devoid of 'embellishments' (Fig. 2). Guiding the reader up the steps into these northern ranges, she explains, 'It is a dark, massive, little-visited corner, this nucleus of Knole.'[1]

Had she turned right at the top of those steps and descended another staircase into the basement, she might have gained a different impression, for the cellar that opens out at the bottom contains a surprise (Fig. 3). On the walls are mural paintings dating from the second half of the 15th century (Fig. 4). On account of their antiquity, typology and location they are, by any estimation, remarkable, but they have never been the subject of scholarly investigation and remain largely unknown. It is the aim of this article to rescue them from the gloom in which they reside and shed some light on their history. Other fragments of Knole's late medieval interiors, including further wall paintings, stained glass and carvings, will also be

considered. This will allow the Knole with which many are acquainted to be glimpsed in an earlier, less-familiar guise as a grand home for the pre-Reformation archbishops of Canterbury.

The main part of the cellar wall painting displays the coats of arms of Thomas Bourchier (*c.* 1411–86), Archbishop of Canterbury from 1454, and members of his immediate family. Bourchier bought Knole in June 1456 from the heir of Sir James Fiennes, Lord Saye and Sele (*c.* 1390–1450).[2] What Bourchier found on his first recorded visit to his new house in March 1459 is unclear, but it is likely that, although Fiennes had begun to build a new house at Knole, its construction had been halted by his death.[3] Bourchier would probably have seen a building site surrounding a few near-complete ranges that were good enough for occasional visits but not yet grand or large enough for a man of his status.

In the immediate weeks following the purchase, Bourchier instructed his workforce to rebuild the house. Although itemised building accounts do not survive for Knole, it is possible to trace the progress of work through the annual accounts of the bailiwick of Otford. They reveal that work began straight away. The account roll for 1455–56 records the purchase of tiles, nails, shingles, lime and

1

2

FIG 2 Knole seen from the north
Photo: © National Trust Images/
John Miller

FIG 3 The buttery cellar below
the north range of Stone Court,
Knole. The wall to the left (the
south side) bears surviving
fragments of late 15th-century
wall paintings
Photo: Ben Blossom, 2016

sand, as well as the wages of carpenters, tilers, plumbers, plasterers and labourers.[4] This makes it clear that the work involved the consolidation of extant buildings. It is likely that this work was aimed at making habitable whatever already existed of Fiennes's house. The work concluded before the end of the decade.

Following a couple of years' break, the workforce returned *en masse*, appearing once again in the 1460–61 accounts. Relatively large payments for building work appear in all the subsequent surviving accounts until 1468, indicating a sustained and transformative phase of construction.[5] Among the handful of craftsmen named in the accounts is Thomas Jurdan (*fl.* 1444–82), a veteran of the royal works at Eton College and later Chief London Bridge Mason and Mason of the King's Works, a role that eventually gave him oversight of the construction of Eltham Palace's great hall.[6] Although none of the accounts describe which of Knole's buildings Jurdan and his colleagues worked on, it is most likely that the

period 1460–68 saw the construction of the ranges surrounding Stone Court, including the northern range, which contains the wall paintings, and the western range, which hosted a new entrance to the house: the imposing Bourchier Tower gatehouse.

A third building phase appears in the accounts covering the years 1472–74. They too record payments to masons and carpenters and also, for the first time, the purchase of substantial quantities of brick.[7] This phase of work probably extended Knole even further west through the addition of the ranges around Green Court and Stable Court that, in the past, have been unconvincingly attributed to later owners, Archbishops Morton (d. 1500) or Warham (*c.* 1450–1532), or Henry VIII (1491–1547).[8] By the early 1470s Bourchier was elderly; his itineraries reveal that he spent increasing amounts of time at Knole, favouring it over Lambeth Palace or any of his other houses. It was to Knole that in old age he effectively retired from court, dying there in 1486. The expansion of the house around Green Court suggests that Knole's new role as a semi-permanent home for an elderly archbishop necessitated more accommodation for staff and guests than it had when it was an occasional stopping place for an itinerant churchman.

The accounts provide useful context and chronology, but they are not able to reveal anything about the interiors during this period. Indeed, the only description of the furnishing or decoration of Knole during the decades in which it belonged to the archbishops of Canterbury comes from the will of Bourchier's successor, William Warham, giving his nephew,

> all of my wall cloths hanging in the chamber in which I sleep at Knole, on which are painted images of Jesus Christ, Saint John the Baptist and some of the other apostles...and also all of my wall cloths in my other chamber next to the chamber in which I sleep at Knole, on which are painted images of hunters with bears, boars and stags.[9]

Many of the interiors at Knole during Bourchier's time must likewise have been decorated with movable hangings – both painted cloth and tapestries. Their ephemeral nature means that they have long since disappeared.

There are, however, surviving fragments of more permanent features from this period, of which the most important are the cellar wall paintings. Although badly damaged by over-painting, plastering and neglect, it is possible to identify three schemes of wall painting, executed in at least two phases. Of these the heraldic scheme is the earliest, best preserved and most easily dateable.

On the south wall of the cellar are four surviving or partly surviving coats of arms. Each is placed within a twisted mantle. Reading the scheme from right to left, first come the Plantagenet royal arms (Fig. 4). Next to them, displayed under a red cardinal's hat, are those of

Archbishop Bourchier himself, comprising his own family arms impaled with the pallium of the see of Canterbury. Third come the arms of the archbishop's father, Sir William Bourchier, impaling the arms of his mother, Anne of Woodstock (Fig. 5). The fourth arms are those of Bourchier's eldest brother, Henry, Earl of Essex, impaled with the arms of his wife, Isabel Langley, daughter of Richard, third Earl of Cambridge.[10] Since Bourchier's eldest brother is represented, it seems likely that the scheme was intended to deliver a dynastic message. The inclusion of the cardinal's hat above the archbishop's arms suggests that it cannot have been painted before his promotion to that rank in September 1467.[11] His death on 30 March 1486 is the *terminus ante quem*.

To the left of the arms, several metres from the shield of the Earl of Essex, is a fragment of a figurative scene (Fig. 6). The scene is in two pieces, separated by an area of damaged plaster, but these should be treated as parts of a single scheme. On the right-hand side is the head of Christ framed by the spandrels of an arch. Flecks of vermilion red on his head suggest blood and indicate that it shows a Man of Sorrows or the Crucifixion. To the left, beyond the damaged plaster, is a kneeling supplicant with his or her hands raised in a gesture of prayer, grief or offering (Fig. 1). The scheme has previously been identified by E. Clive Rouse as the Martyrdom of Thomas Becket, but in truth there is not enough remaining from which to draw that conclusion.[12] Indeed, it is more likely a depiction of the dying or risen Christ surrounded by mourners.

Analysis of the paint and plaster stratigraphy by Tobit Curteis suggests that the figurative scene is on the same layer of plaster as the heraldry. It is most likely, therefore, that the figurative painting likewise dates from the last decades of Bourchier's life.[13] Curteis's survey further demonstrates that a third element in the painting scheme – a foliate frieze reminiscent of late medieval northern European grotesque work – is on plaster that overlays the heraldic and figurative schemes and is, therefore, a later addition. It is possible that it is the last surviving fragment of a scheme that originally covered the older painting entirely. Unlike the earlier schemes, which are visible only on the south wall of the cellar, the frieze is also traceable on the north and east walls, suggesting that the cellar was once decorated throughout.

The cellar itself is long, low ceilinged and gloomy, despite being lit from the north by small windows (Fig. 3). In the centre of the northern wall is a door providing access to Queen's Court – a service courtyard – but the space was also formerly accessed via a staircase descending from the buttery at the end of the Great Hall. It seems an unlikely space to find wall paintings. However, a closer look at the execution and materials of the paintings reveals that they are not of the highest calibre. They are not, for example, comparable in quality to the contemporary wall paintings at Eton College, or to earlier paintings at Westminster Abbey and the Tower of London. Instead, they seem to be by a competent but otherwise unremarkable painter using the most basic and cheapest of pigments. Although pigment analysis has not been undertaken, it is clear from inspection that the palette is restricted to red,

4

5

yellow, white and black. The blue to be expected in the quarters of the royal arms (Fig. 4) is noticeably absent, presumably because it would have required much more expense. As a whole, the images constitute a vernacular type of wall painting, not unlike those that were once common in parish churches and middling-status houses, such as Bradley Manor, Devon, and Cothay Manor, Somerset.[14]

Although the wall paintings are not of the finest quality, they nonetheless demonstrate that the room held a significant function over an extended period of time.

FIG 4 Part of the scheme of wall paintings in the buttery cellar at Knole, showing the Plantagenet royal arms surrounded by a twisted mantle
Photo: Ben Blossom, 2016

FIG 5 Part of the scheme of wall paintings in the buttery cellar at Knole, showing the arms of the Archbishop of Canterbury, Thomas Bourchier (right), and those of his parents, Sir William Bourchier and Anne of Woodstock (left)
Photo: Ben Blossom, 2016

6

Given the connection with the buttery it seems likely that it was a continuation of it. It is thus best described as a buttery cellar. The main function of such a room was storage, principally for beer but perhaps also for wine, but there is evidence that cellars could act as entertaining spaces as well. Household ordinances that were drawn up in the early 16th century for Archbishop Cranmer (1489–1556) include an instruction to the butlers of the cellar that eating and drinking were permitted in the cellar, 'yf it be for a straunger for my Lordes honour'.[15] In other words, the provision of hospitality to the archbishop's guests was not restricted to the great hall and state chambers, but could be extended into the cellar itself. The room therefore served as a place where guests could draw their refreshment directly from the barrel. The wall paintings added a touch of colour to the space while also delivering two important messages. The first was presumably moralistic, but the substantial loss of detail from the figurative scheme means that it is difficult to identify its true meaning. The second, delivered heraldically, was almost certainly intended to remind the archbishop's guests of whose hospitality they were partaking.

Bourchier's personal heraldic badges dominate Knole's other late medieval interiors. Within the same range, two storeys above the cellar, a much smaller wall painting survives. In the window soffit of a garderobe that served a suite of guest lodgings is a repeating stencilled pattern of oak leaves in red ochre. Again, the scheme shows some similarity with the repeated fleur-de-lis pattern at Bradley Manor. Oak leaves, though a relatively common decorative motif, in this instance seem to have held a specific heraldic meaning and to have been adopted by the archbishop as one of several personal badges. The symbol represented Bourchier's maternal lineage and was derived from the badge of his grandfather Thomas of Woodstock, which depicted a stock of oak with its leaves.[16]

Oak leaves are in evidence elsewhere too. A leaded casement window on the first floor of the Duke's Tower retains quarries of stained glass that alternate oak leaves with Bourchier's other badge, the more familiar double knot. The casement itself is of a later design so those quarries were evidently reused from elsewhere. They may have come from the oriel window that lights the chamber over the Bourchier Tower gate, which retains similar fragments of stained glass. This chamber was once part of a suite of rooms for important guests or high-ranking household officers. For the most part, the oriel is now glazed with clear glass, but the top-most dagger in the tracery and the two cusps on either side retain *in situ* stained glass, which suggests that the glazing of the whole window was once more elaborate. Again, they have a heraldic theme: the cusps display the Bourchier knot while the dagger shows a falcon or an eagle (Fig. 8). This image also appears among other heraldic badges on the font at St Mary the Virgin, Mortlake, and in contemporary stained glass at Canterbury Cathedral. Both were also commissioned by Bourchier. Furthermore, a drawing of a similar bird appears in a 15th-century book of heraldic badges at the British Library, where it is labelled in a contemporary hand, 'my lord Canterbery'.[17] The maker of the stained glass may have been John Forte, a London glazier who was paid £8 19s 9½d according to the accounts for 1460–61.[18]

The ceiling of the oriel chamber is supported by two stone corbels, each in the shape of a shield. One is carved with religious imagery, in the form of a six-pointed star surrounding the letters 'IHR', while the Bourchier double knot appears on the other. Here it frames the word 'Mercy', the M of which is formed by two entwined dragons (Fig. 7). Just as in the cellar, the message here is both dynastic and designed to remind the occupants that they were recipients of Bourchier's goodwill.

Knole retains two further fragments of its once-grand medieval interior. Although neither is now *in situ*, they demonstrate that this heraldic message was repeated elsewhere. The first is a piece of carved wood reused in the much-altered chapel screen. It bears the motto '*Benedictus Deus*' surmounted by oak leaves. The second is a fireplace lintel that has been in store since the mid 20th century, but which formerly graced the first-floor chamber of the Duke's Tower. This room may have been the archbishop's own bedchamber. In the spandrels of the fireplace are the pallium of Canterbury and, again, the Bourchier double knot. Between the spandrels the motto '*Benedictus Deus*' is repeated. This fireplace is notable as being the only surviving 15th-century example at Knole to bear anything more elaborate than simple moulding profiles.

What remains of Knole's late medieval decorative interiors is only a tiny fragment of what must once have been lavish ornamentation. Nonetheless, the proliferation of Bourchier's personal badges, most especially where they are paired with those of his close kin, is worthy of further remark. Through a display of family symbols, Bourchier seems to have been tying the identity of the house to that of his lineage more strongly than to that of the archbishopric. Complex motivations underlay this, but it must in part have related to Bourchier's understanding of Knole's status. Although he bought Knole in 1456, two years after being elevated to the archiepiscopacy, it was not until 1480 that he officially granted it to the see for the perpetual use of his successors.[19] Prior to that, it was legally his own house.

The separation that this afforded it from the archiepiscopal estates was probably beneficial given the unstable politics of the second half of the 15th century. Bourchier, like his brothers, favoured York over Lancaster, though he was politically astute enough to retain his archbishopric under both houses. It is of particular note that the three identified periods of construction at Knole – 1456, 1460–68 and 1472–74 – correspond broadly with the years of Yorkist ascendency. This pattern hints at Bourchier's uncertainty about the security of his position. To counter this, he invested Knole with a special status, seeking to identify it as his own house and not part of his official estate. Had he been forced to abdicate his archiepiscopal throne – an unprecedented but not inconceivable possibility, considering that in 1456 he had been deposed as Lord Chancellor of England and subsequently arrested and imprisoned by Lancastrian ministers – Knole would have offered him a place of refuge and a house that, barring attainder, would have remained his own.[20] Those small fragments of Knole's medieval interiors point to this duality. It was here, behind the protective veil of its walls, that Bourchier could await whatever fate time and politics held for him while enjoying the trappings of luxury that his wealth and status offered.

Alden Gregory is Curator of Historic Buildings at Historic Royal Palaces. He wrote his DPhil thesis on the architectural and social history of Knole under the archbishops of Canterbury in the 15th and early 16th centuries.

ACKNOWLEDGEMENTS
This article arises from research undertaken by me in completion of my doctoral thesis, 'Knole: An Architectural and Social History of the Archbishop of Canterbury's House, 1456–1538', University of Sussex, 2010. The thesis was made possible by Collaborative Doctoral Award funding from the AHRC and the support of the University of Sussex and the National Trust. I would like to express my thanks to all those who supported this research. I am especially grateful to the AHRC, the staff and volunteers of the National Trust, in particular Emma Slocombe and Helen Fawbert, and to Robert, Jane and Bridget Sackville-West, Professor Maurice Howard and Dr Edward Town.

1. Vita Sackville-West, *Knole and the Sackvilles*, London, 1922, pp. 1, 5.
2. Kent History and Library Centre, U1450 T4/17.
3. Lambeth Palace Library (hereafter LPL), Reg. Bourchier, f. 76r.
4. The National Archives (hereafter TNA) SC6 1129/4.
5. LPL, ED 1243; TNA, SC 6/1129/7; TNA, SC 6/1129/8; TNA, SC 6/1129/9; LPL, ED 543; TNA, SC 6/1130/1; LPL, ED 1348.
6. LPL, ED 1243, f. 10; John Harvey, 'Jurdan, Thomas [Jordan] (*fl.* 1444–1482)', in *English Medieval Architects: A Biographical Dictionary down to 1550*, Gloucester, 1987, p. 165.
7. TNA, SC 6/1130/4; TNA, SC 6/1130/5.
8. Anthony Emery, *Greater Medieval Houses of England and Wales: Southern England*, Cambridge, 2006, p. 368; Howard Colvin (ed.), *The History of the King's Works, 1485-1660*, London, 1982, p. 218; P.A. Faulkner, 'Some Medieval Archiepiscopal Palaces', *The Archaeological Journal*, vol. CXXVII, 1971, pp. 145-46.
9. TNA, PROB/11/24. The word 'painted' has been translated from the ambiguous Latin *pinguntur*, which may also be translated as 'embellished'.
10. I should like to record my gratitude to the late Richard Leathes who was a dedicated volunteer at Knole and a great source of knowledge about historic heraldry. Conversations with Richard about the heraldic scheme in the cellars were of great help in the completion of my study.
11. Linda Clark, 'Bourchier, Thomas (*c.* 1411–1486)', *Oxford Dictionary of National Biography*, Oxford, 2004 [accessed 24 February 2016: http://www.oxforddnb.com/view/article/2993].
12. E. Clive Rouse, 'Painted Decoration at Knole, Kent', unpublished report, 1977.
13. Tobit Curteis, 'Knole, Kent: Preliminary Survey of the Wall Paintings in the Stone Court Cellar', unpublished report, 3 March 2010, p. 5.
14. Emery, op. cit., pp. 501, 532.
15. LPL, MS 884, f. 14.
16. M.P. Siddons, *Heraldic Badges in England and Wales*, 3 vols., Woodbridge, 2009, vol. II, pt. II, p. 41.
17. British Library, Add. Ms. 40742, f. 6.
18. LPL, ED 1243.
19. Canterbury Cathedral Archives, Reg. S, ff. 313–13v.
20. Clark, op. cit. [accessed 24 February 2016: http://www.oxforddnb.com/view/article/2993]

FIG 7 Heraldic corbel in the Bourchier Tower room at Knole, which dates to the 1460s
Photo: Ben Blossom, 2016

FIG 8 Stained glass from the Bourchier Tower oriel at Knole, which dates to the 1460s and may have been made by the glazier John Forte
Photo: Ben Blossom, 2016

7

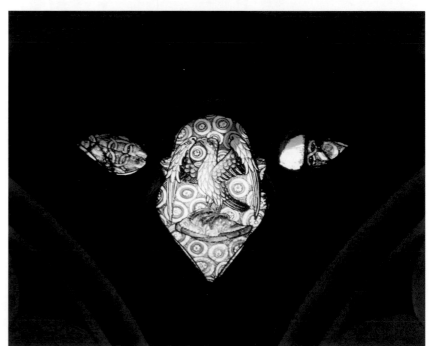

8

THE BIRD HOUSE AT KNOLE

A CABINET OF CURIOUS BIRDS

Private menageries of exotic birds and animals can sometimes seem like oddities in the landscape. But, as CAMILLA BERESFORD explains, the Bird House at Knole is a well-documented example, whose structure and contents deserve to be studied

THE BIRD HOUSE AT KNOLE is a mid 18th-century gothic curiosity set in a garden partially surrounded by sham ruins near the middle of the 15th-century deer park (Fig. 1). In its heyday it housed a magnificent collection of exotic birds. The opening of trade routes across the world in the 17th and 18th centuries brought exotic objects, flora and fauna on to the market, provoking curiosity and satisfying the desire for new things. One consequence was that a number of 18th-century landowners with a passion for collecting and an interest in the scientific discoveries of the Enlightenment adorned their estates with menageries. The display of birds and animals in purpose-built rooms, buildings or gardens gave such men and women great prestige and added lustre to their reputations. The Bird House at Knole was a typical example.

Lionel Cranfield Sackville (1688–1765), created Duke of Dorset in 1720, inherited Knole shortly after his 18th birthday. It became his principal seat in 1709 following his marriage to the courtier Elizabeth Colyear (1686–1768) and his appointments as Lord Warden of the Cinque

Ports and Lieutenant of Dover Castle.[1] The engraving *Knowle in the Parish of Sevenoaks in Kent* by Johannes Kip after Leonard Knyff, published in *Britannia Illustrata* (1707), provides a bird's-eye view of the landscape he inherited.[2] The main features were the palatial house and the garden, which was enclosed by high late medieval walls. Beyond these, to the east, were a prominent tree-topped knoll and a cluster of buildings operating as the park lodge. A walk along the north side of the perimeter wall of the gardens was directly aligned with this knoll at the east end and with the planting on a hillock known as Echo Mount at the west end.

In the 1710s the gardens received most of the duke's attention and it was not until the 1720s that work properly started on the park. The exception was the knoll east of the walled garden, which became known as Chestnut Mount. It appears in the engraving *West Prospect of Knole* by John Harris after Thomas Badeslade.[3] The engraving shows that the knoll, marked with the letter D, was planted with two circles of trees. The border contains the observation 'From

FIG 1 The Bird House in the deer park at Knole, Kent
Photo: Ben Blossom, 2016

2

the Mount D is seen a very fine prospect'. The rings of two massive chestnut trees that fell here in the Great Storm of 1987 show that the trees dated from the early 1700s. The work on the park in the 1720s included the creation of a new walled garden next to the lodge and a new mount on land taken in at the southern end of the park in 1724. The Broad Ride, a clearing through an oak and beech wood, led from the new mount to Chestnut Mount, with which it was directly aligned. Three walks were made on Chestnut Mount, which was planted with furze and equipped with a raddle fence (made of flexible green twigs or sticks, interwoven between upright posts to make a hedge). Walks were also laid out between it and the walled gardens.[4]

The Duke of Dorset was appointed Lord Lieutenant of Ireland in 1730, serving there until 1737. During this time he returned to England each summer after the parliamentary session had ended. Some work was carried out during this period and in 1735 Lieutenant Colonel John

3

Campbell (*c.* 1693–1770) advised on changes to the gardens.[5] Records relating to work undertaken in the park in 1733–34 show the beginnings of a menagerie, which at this point was housed near the lodge on the west side of the walled kitchen garden:

> paid a haggler for bringing the Swans from Southend, and for getting ant eggs for the pheasants. And for making some alteration in the keepers garden, and helping the carpenter make a reed hedge in the antelopes lodge. Paid for fifteen bundles of hurdle rods to make wings for the hutches.[6]

A garden planted with oak, yew and laurel was made for the antelopes during this period. At the same time, a ha-ha was created 'by the Garden wall next the lodge plain', opening up the view towards the kitchen garden and Chestnut Mount. In 1737 the 'furzy part of the sand hole by the chestnut mount' was planted with 'red & white elder trees'.[7] In 1738 hens were bought to 'set Dutch & pheasant eggs' and a payment was made to 'Kemble the healer for bringing the bantam Fowls from London'.[8]

The duke served a second term as Lord Lieutenant of Ireland from 1750 to 1755. By 1755, the formal 17th- and early 18th-century layout at Knole would have been outmoded. Although he would have known that such things had gone out of fashion, the duke kept the axial planting within the park. Nevertheless, the duke attempted to capture something of the Arcadian style – to which the ancient timber, natural topography and far-reaching views were ideally suited – by breaking up some of the avenues and planting trees on a massive scale to soften the formal lines. While in general he chose not to fill the park with what Edmund Burke would later call 'foppish structures of this enlightened age', he did create a small number of these at Chestnut Mount.[9] A miniature landscape was laid out in the 1750s, containing all the requisite features of fashionable mid to late 18th-century gardens: a gothic building, a grotto, ruins, a menagerie, an aviary, vistas and a circuit walk following a serpentine course.

The Bird House was placed at the centre point of the clearing along the Broad Walk. It could be viewed from the clairvoyée and ha-ha at the east end of the garden. Work on it was underway in 1754, when the Reverend Richard Pococke wrote: 'In a shelter'd situation in the park, near the garden, they are making a nonagon building, it is to be a sort of cottage, where poultry of all kinds are to be kept, in which the Dutchess delights'.[10] Thomas Benge Burr gave more details in *The History of Tunbridge Wells*, published in 1766, by which time the building had been completed and the collection of birds started:

'the duke has lately erected a little gothic hermitage…at a small distance from the house, which is a great curiosity in itself, as well as on account of the vast variety of uncommon birds &c that are kept there'. The exact list of specimens is not known, but menageries at this period (for example, at Osterley, Bulstrode and Frogmore) typically housed beautiful native birds, such as pheasants, doves, partridges, hens, geese and ducks, along with exotic and rare birds, such as macaws, parrots and parakeets, and some larger species, such as storks, cranes, peacocks and possibly birds of prey (Fig. 2). Aquatic birds would have had access to the ponds between the Bird House and the kitchen garden. A manuscript from the 1750s in the Sackville papers gives details of one type of bird housed there:

> Directions to feed Storks: The Storks must be fed with small Eels or Grigs [crickets or grasshoppers], the Drawings of Fowles or Sheep's Livers – raw or any other raw meat – Small Frogs they are very fond of & must have a tub or pan of water constantly by them to drink & wash themselves in – In the winter they must be kept in a Stable or warm shed.[11] (Fig. 3)

The Bird House as it survives is a nine-sided building. An entrance porch and a pair of small towers form three projections. The building today is little changed from the one shown in a pen-and-wash drawing by the Flemish landscape painter Hendrik de Cort (1742–1810), apart from the absence of a spire, the rough render and the relocation of the entrance from the east to the north side (Fig. 4).[12] The de Cort view also shows the landscaping around the Bird House. At the time the drawing was made, the Bird House had a grass clearing in front of it on the south and east sides and a building behind it to the north. Another building or wall, possibly part of the 'ruins', was situated to the north-east. In the background of the drawing, the rising ground to the north is shown planted with a mixture of conifers and deciduous trees. In the foreground are some shrubs. The curve of the path on the east side of the garden is also apparent.

An Ordnance Survey map published in 1869 (Fig. 5) shows the Bird House and three smaller buildings to the north of it: a partly extant grotto; an extant building that probably accommodated birds and animals on the ground floor and a dove house on the first floor; and between them another building that was possibly used for storage.[13] The map shows a serpentine path running around the perimeter of the mount.

Some of the buildings seen in the de Cort view and on the Ordnance Survey map were described by John H. Brady in *The Visitor's Guide to Knole* (1839):

> To the south-east of the extensive pleasure-grounds at the back of the mansion, is a small building, in the ecclesiastic style of pointed architecture, surrounded by palisades, and a broken flint wall. Its shape is multi-angular, having gables and a pointed roof, finished with a lofty spire, and its rooms are very irregularly formed … Scattered about are the apparent remains of the foundations of buildings of a date considerably prior

4

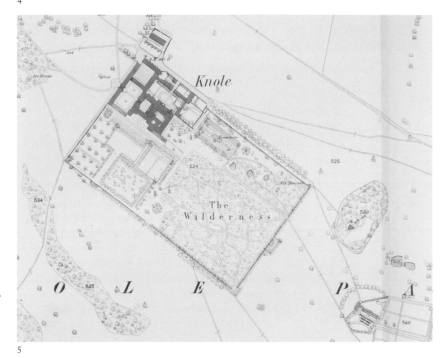

5

to the dwelling. The stone door and window frames have quite the appearance of antiquity, and were no doubt brought here at the demolition of some ancient building in the neighbourhood. These erections were made under the direction of Captain Smyth, (father of Sir Sydney Smyth), who resided much at Knole… the materials were probably brought from Otford, as a tower, forming a portion of the old palace, was at that period taken down…A small collection of foreign birds was then placed here, secured within netted compartments; a dove-house, and conveniences for rearing and keeping poultry were made.

The ruins around the southern end of the Bird House garden were probably added when Captain Smith (or Smyth; d. 1804) stayed at Knole in or around 1760.[14] Smith had been aide-de-camp to Lieutenant General Lord George Sackville (1716–85), the first duke's third and favourite son. Sackville was court-martialled for refusing to

FIG 4 *Knole: The Aviary*, c. 1790–1810, Hendrik de Cort, pen and ink with grey wash over pencil, 33.7 x 49.6cm, Royal Collection Trust © HM Queen Elizabeth II, 2016

FIG 5 Detail from the 1st edition of the Ordnance Survey, 25" to the mile, 1869, showing the oval-shaped knoll, with the mount to the north and the nine-sided Bird House to the south
Photo: courtesy the author

The Marine Villa of JOHN SMITH ESQ^r. *(Father of SIR SYDNEY SMITH)* under Dover Cliffs.

Engraved by Rawle from an original Drawing by John Nixon Esqr

Published by J.Sewell Cornhill Mar: 2.28.01.

6

FIG 6 *The Marine Villa of John Smith Esqr. (Father of Sir Sydney Smith) under Dover Cliffs*, 1801, Samuel Rawle after a drawing by John Nixon, engraving on paper, 12.5 x 19cm, private collection

order an attack in the closing phase of the Battle of Minden in August 1759. Smith was the only officer who witnessed the event to support him. The duke was grateful for Smith's support for his son and rewarded him with a gift of land near Dover and on Sevenoaks Common.[15] Some of these ruins are extant today. At the east entrance, stretches of wall appear on either side of a large arch. To the north are the fragmentary ruins of a building and a small ruined tower. After retiring from his position as an usher in Queen Charlotte's household, Smith built a summer residence under Dover Cliffs, consisting of a series of buildings with gothic windows and roofs made of upturned boats, connected by passages to caves cut in the rock (Fig. 6).[16]

The passion for collecting and displaying flora and fauna was not new in the 18th century. Physic gardens were established at Oxford in 1621 and Chelsea in 1673. Antiquarians such as Elias Ashmole (1617–92) and William Courten (1642–1702) collected and displayed items of natural history alongside works of art, jewels, miniatures and antiquities in cabinets of curiosities and private museums. There had been famous royal collections of animals for centuries at Woodstock and the Tower of London. Curiosities were often advertised in the press, becoming the talk of the coffee houses. John Evelyn described an outing to St James's Park, where he saw 'various animals, and examined the throat of ye "Onocratylus", or Pelican, a fowle between a Stork and a Swan, a melancholy waterfowl brought from Astracan by the Russian Ambassador'.[17] In his diaries Samuel Pepys wrote of visits to see Crowly the lion in the Tower Menagerie, a 'great variety of fowl which I never saw before' in St James's Park and 'a fine rarity: of fishes kept in a glass of water, that will live so for ever; and finely marked they are, being foreign.'[18] The development of menageries in aristocratic English landscapes offered an opportunity to enlighten and be

enlightened. One of the earliest aristocratic menageries was created by the second Duke of Richmond at Goodwood. By 1725, it contained lions, a tiger, an eagle, an ostrich and bears. In general, however, collections in the 18th century tended not to include large carnivores, but consisted mostly of exotic birds, with possibly some small mammals or herbivorous quadrupeds.

Women as well as men made collections in cabinets, botanical gardens and menageries. At a time when their voices could not be heard in many arenas, they were able to make their mark in this quasi-domestic sphere. Sir Hans Sloane (1660–1753) benefitted from the herbarium of his neighbour in Chelsea, the botanist and gardener Mary Somerset, Duchess of Beaufort (1630–1715), and Horace Walpole's collections at Strawberry Hill contained the 'spoils of many renowned cabinets; as Dr Mead's, lady Elizabeth Germaine's, lord Oxford's, the duchess of Portland's, and of about forty more celebrity'.[19] The Duchess of Portland had the largest natural history collection of the time, housed in the Portland Museum at Bulstrode.[20] The duchess also had a menagerie and a Chinese dairy, which were thought

exceedingly well worth seeing, for the Dutchess of Portland is as eager in collecting animals, as if she foresaw another deluge, and was assembling every creature after its kind, to preserve the species: she used to be very happy in a great variety of fowls, which is a very fortunate taste.[21]

The Bulstrode menagerie contained silver, gold and pied pheasants, a peacock pheasant, a crown bird, a stork and a red-legged partridge. The smaller birds included finches, Java sparrows, Virginia nightingales and tumblers.[22] Mary Delany remarked, 'Surely an application to natural beauties must enlarge the mind?[23] Delany and the Duchess of Portland were both members of the Bluestockings Circle, which had been set up to support and encourage women in their intellectual pursuits.[24]

Mid 18th-century menageries usually featured a centrally placed building, often circular or polygonal, with windows giving views out over the surrounding gardens, to which the larger birds had free access when released from their pens. Smaller songbirds were kept in aviaries. Many of the menagerie buildings featured a room downstairs in which to take tea and a room upstairs for the keeper, and this seems to have been the case at Knole.[25] The style of the buildings in this period was usually gothic or Chinese, but a classical style was later used by the architect Robert Adam (1728–92) in the parks designed by Lancelot Brown (1716–83). These buildings were more usually positioned against the boundary of the menagerie and were sometimes double-sided, giving access to a garden with a different function on the other side. The gothic polygonal design of the Knole Bird House, centrally positioned within its garden, was therefore typical of menageries of its time. More unusual was the spire, although a similar feature was part of Richard Bentley's plan for the Priory of St Hubert's – an ornamental model farm designed for Henrietta Howard, Countess of Suffolk (1689–1767) at Marble Hill, Twickenham – in the 1750s.

The mid 18th century also saw the appearance of a number of books on birds, illustrated with beautifully coloured plates. The seminal work of this sort was *A Natural History of Uncommon Birds* by the naturalist George Edwards (1694–1773), which was published between 1743 and 1751 (Fig. 7). The first published account of a private collection of birds was *Portraits of Rare and Curious Birds, with their descriptions, from the Menagery of Osterly Park* (1794–99) by the artist and ornithologist William Hayes (1735–1802).[26] The Irish watercolour artist Samuel Dixon (*fl.* 1748–69) produced a set of 12 basso-relievo bird pictures sold in japanned frames from 1750. Each picture bore a dedication on the reverse: a goldfinch with honeysuckle and ranunculus was dedicated, surely not coincidentally, to the Duchess of Dorset. Porcelain, wallpaper and silk fabrics produced in the 1750s often featured a combination of exotic Chinese birds and flowers in rocky landscapes. Vincennes and Sèvres porcelain picked up on these motifs. Examples dating from the 1750s at Knole may have been purchased for use at the Bird House.

Collectors would often exchange birds and animals among themselves. Most of the professional suppliers were based in London. New arrivals were advertised to be 'Sold and Seen'.[27] The most prestigious of the suppliers was probably Joshua Brookes, who had several menagerie shops (Fig. 8). One of his sons, Paul, travelled the world to find new flora and fauna and another son, Joshua, was a surgeon-anatomist. His anatomy school in Great Marlborough Street had a private museum and a small menagerie. We do not know who supplied the Knole

birds, but Brookes's Menagerie was one probable source.[28] This business also supplied birds and animals to Goodwood during the late 18th century.[29]

The menagerie of birds continued to operate at Knole into the early 19th century: the Bailiff's Memorandum and Corn Book show allowances of wheat and barley for the poultry at the Bird House in 1813–15.[30] By 1839, however, it had been converted to residential use: the 1841 census shows the 'Bird House, Knole Park' occupied by William Webb, an agricultural labourer, and his wife. At the time of the 1881 census, it was occupied by George Tooy, a park keeper and widower, who lived there with his five children and a servant. The 1889 *Guide to Knole House* stated that the Bird House had been 'until lately … enclosed, and a small quantity of foreign birds and fancy poultry kept here. A few peacocks, which roost in the very fine cedar near, are about all that remaining'.[31]

FIG 7 A peacock pheasant, plate 67 in George Edwards' *A Natural History of Uncommon Birds*, part II, London, 1747
© The British Library Board

7

During the early decades of the 19th century, interest in private collections of birds and animals faded. The buildings used to house them were demolished or converted to other uses. They were often turned into residences, as at Knole, or became game larders and gashouses, or were left as follies. As landowners' interests turned to practical husbandry and ornamental poultry yards, model farms and dairies became features in private parks. Brookes's Menagerie closed in 1820 after more than 60 years in business and the collection was sold.[32] Memories of private menageries are now largely lost, although the label sometimes lingers on in the name of a field or wood, perhaps marked on an old map. The surviving buildings are now seen as little more than oddities. Vita Sackville-West described the Bird House at Knole as a 'queer little sham Gothic house… which always frightened me as a child because I thought it looked like the witch's house in Hansel and Gretel, tucked away in its hollow, with its pointed gables'.[33]

Camilla Beresford is a consultant landscape architect and historian, covering all aspects of landscape history with a particular interest in multi-phased landscapes and topographical art.

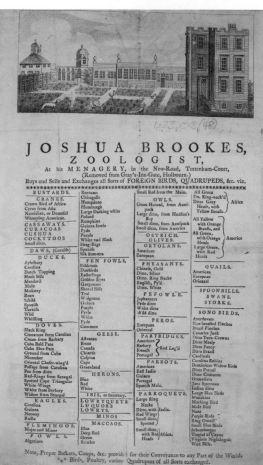

1. Elizabeth Colyear (d. 1768) was the daughter of Lieutenant-General Walter Philip Colyear (c. 1657–1747), governor of Bonn and then Namur. She was a maid of honour to Queen Anne from 1703 to 1714 and later First Lady of the Bedchamber and Mistress of the Robes to Caroline of Ansbach, wife of George II.
2. *Britannia Illustrata or views of several of the Queen's Palaces, as also of the principal Seats of the Nobility and Gentry of Great Britain*, London, 1707.
3. Published in John Harris, *History of Kent*, London, 1719.
4. Kent History and Library Centre (hereafter KHLC), U269 A301/1.
5. Lieutenant Colonel John Campbell (1693–1770), later fourth Duke of Argyll, purchased Combe Bank on the edge of Sevenoaks in 1720 and commissioned Roger Morris to build a new house in 1721. Campbell was linked to several members of the Burlington Circle, including Alexander Pope and William Kent, and may have provided advice on the park as well as the gardens.
6. KHLC, U269 A301/1.
7. KHLC, U269 A301/1. The sand hole had been formed by quarrying sand and was on the southeast side of the mount.
8. KHLC, U269 A49.
9. Letter from Edmund Burke to the third Duke of Dorset, 14 September 1791, quoted in Robert Sackville-West, *Inheritance: The Story of Knole and the Sackvilles*, London, 2010.
10. James Joel Cartwright (ed.), *The Travels through England of Dr. Richard Pococke, successively Bishop of Meath and of Ossory, during 1750, 1751, and later years*, Camden Society, New Series vol. XLIV, London, 1889.
11. KHLC, U269/E23/3 (Bdl. 83).
12. Royal Collection, RCIN 917963. Published in A.P. Oppé, *English Drawings: Stuart and Georgian periods in the collection of His Majesty The King at Windsor Castle*, London, 1950. De Cort specialised in topographical paintings of the estates of the British nobility, for which he usually prepared wash drawings prior to full paintings if commissioned. See also notes to lot 64, Hendrik de Cort, *View of Chelsea Farm*, in Christies sale 6956, 'British Pictures 1500–1850', 2004.
13. Ordnance Survey, Kent sheet 40.1, 1 mile to 6 inches, 1871 (surveyed 1869).
14. Captain Smith built a gothic house called Ashgrove on Sevenoaks Common in c. 1760, since remodelled and now West Heath School.
15. KHLC, U269 M172.
16. James Dugdale referred to this building as follows: 'Below the castle hill, on the sea beach, is a remarkable villa belonging to Sir W. Sidney Smith, by whose father, Captain Smith, Aid-de-Camp to Lord Sackville, at the battle of Minden, it was erected. It is composed of flints and chalk, and consists of different low buildings, inclosing a small court. In its general aspect, it resembles a fort. The roofing is composed of inverted sea-boats, of the largest size, strongly pitched over.' James Dugdale, *The New British Traveller: Or Modern Panorama of England and Wales*, 4 vols., London, 1819, vol. III, p. 178–79.
17. John Evelyn's diary entry for 29 March 1665 in William Bray (ed), *Memoirs illustrative of the Life and Writings of John Evelyn Esq*, 2 vols., London, 1819, vol. I.
18. Entries for 11 January 1660, 18 August 1661, and 28 May 1665 [accessed 16 April 2016: www.pepysdiary.com].
19. Horace Walpole, *The Duchess of Portland's Museum*, New York, 1936.
20. Most of the collection was sold after her death in 1786 in 4,156 lots over 38 days. See *A Catalogue of the Portland Museum, lately the Property of the Duchess Dowager of Portland, deceased: which will be sold by auction by Mr. Skinner & Co. on Monday, the 24th day of April, 1786*. The 'Exceeding Curious Articles' included the Barberini head of Jupiter Serapis, purchased by Lord Walpole (lot 4154), and the Portland or Barberini Vase, now in the British Museum (lot 4155).
21. Elizabeth Montagu (Robinson) to Gilbert West, 2 March 1752, printed in Matthew Montagu (ed.), *The Letters of Mrs. Elizabeth Montagu: Part the Second*, London, 1813.
22. From a description by Caroline Powys in 1769, quoted in Caroline Grigson, *Menagerie: The History of Exotic Animals in England*, Oxford, 2016, p. 129.
23. Mrs Delany to Miss Dewes, 4 October 1768, printed in Augusta Llanover (ed.), *The Autobiography and Correspondence of Mary Granville, Mrs Delany*, London, 1862.
24. Mary Delany had made a famous grotto at Delville, outside Dublin, in the 1730s and was acquainted with the Duke of Dorset from their time in Dublin. She later produced a series of botanical collages that are now in the British Museum.
25. KHLC, U269 E4. An inventory drawn up in 1765 referred to a Dutch tea kettle, eight tea cups and saucers, a Dutch coffeepot and six coffee cups there, as well as tables, chairs and cushions.
26. See also KHLC, U269/Z26, a prospectus of 1769 in the Sackville papers for the publication of Hayes's book *A natural history of British birds, &c with their portraits, accurately drawn, and beautifully coloured from nature, by Mr Hayes*, London, 1775.
27. Advertisements were placed in the *Public Advertiser* in the 1760s by Brookes, City, and Exeter Change menageries to highlight new arrivals.
28. The history of menageries is the subject of Christopher Plumb, *The Georgian Menagerie: Exotic Animals in Eighteenth-Century London*, London, 2015 and Grigson, op. cit.
29. West Sussex Record Office, PHA/8046; PHA/8049; PHA/8052; PHA/8053; PHA/8054; PHA/8056; PHA/8060; PHA/8305.
30. KHLC, U269/A557.
31. *Guide to Knole House, its State Rooms, Pictures, and Antiquities, with an Account of the Possessors and Park of Knole*, Scarborough, 1889.
32. *The Times*, 11 July 1820.
33. Vita Sackville-West, *Knole and the Sackvilles*, London, 1922 (paperback ed., 1973), p. 39.

FIG 8 *Joshua Brookes Zoologist, at his Menagery in the New-Road Tottenham Court*, 1775
© The British Library Board

1

THE RELUCTANT HEIR
EDWARD SACKVILLE-WEST AT KNOLE

*Edward Sackville–West has long been overshadowed by his cousin Vita, who
was passionately devoted to Knole. But, as EMMA SLOCOMBE explains, his
interiors, furnishings and correspondence, which are to be displayed in public for
the first time, reveal a complex and fascinating personality*

2

FIG 1 (PREVIOUS PAGE) *Edward Sackville-West, c.* 1930, Barbara Ker-Seymer (1905–93), photographic print, 23 x 30cm, Knole, Kent (Sackville Collection) Photo: Richard Holttum, 2016

FIG 2 Photograph showing the West Range and Gatehouse Tower from Green Court, published in *Country Life*, 5 May 1912 Photo: © Country Life

FIG 3 *Vita Sackville-West, c.* 1930, by Lemay, inscribed 'For Eddy from Vita', photographic print, 36 x 28cm, Knole, Kent (Sackville Collection) Photo: Richard Holttum, 2016

THE ENTRANCE TO KNOLE FROM THE PARK is marked by an imposing late medieval Gatehouse Tower in the centre of a sombre façade built of Kentish ragstone. Its gables are decorated with the heraldic leopards of the Sackville family. As visitors pass through two great oak doors, their attention is immediately drawn to the expanse of Green Court, overlooked by the central clock tower topped with a gold weathervane, and to a second, earlier gatehouse that leads to Stone Court and the network of richly furnished apartments that lie beyond. If they were to pause, they might see a small door to their right. This serves as the entrance to a stone spiral staircase that leads to the rooms and the roof above (Fig. 2). The history of the Gatehouse Tower is an unremarkable one, marked by lengthy periods of abandonment and neglect.[1] However, for a brief time, between 1926 and 1940, it formed part of the apartment of Edward Sackville-West (1901–65; Fig. 1), heir to Knole and the Sackville barony.

An accomplished novelist, biographer and music critic, Sackville-West was also a champion of many British artists, composers and literary figures during the interwar and post-war years, some of whom he counted as friends and entertained at Knole, recording their visits in *The Gatehouse, Knole: Visitors Book*. Until recently, Sackville-West has figured as something of a footnote in the history of the family, eclipsed by his well-known cousin, the poet and gardener Vita Sackville-West (1892–1963; Fig. 3), who was born at Knole. The surviving fragments of his interiors, furnishings and collections have been largely overlooked. This year sees the public opening of the Gatehouse Tower for the first time. Through personal photographs, furniture, books and the correspondence and diaries of those closest to him, the displays in the Gate-

3

house Tower rooms will attempt to capture something of Sackville-West's presence at the house.

Edward Charles Sackville-West was born on 13 November 1901, the son of Major Charles John Sackville-West (1870–1962) and his first wife, Maude Bell (1873–1920). Although at birth he was the likely heir to Knole, his relationship with the house as a young child was a relatively distant one.[2] While he and his younger sister Diana (1906–75) were growing up, their father pursued a professional military career that was by nature itinerant, and Sackville-West felt most settled when at his mother's family home, Bourne Park in Kent, a spacious early 18th-century brick mansion set in a landscaped park.[3] The vast expanse of Knole provided something of a contrast. He made occasional visits as the guest of his elderly, unmarried great-uncle Lionel Sackville-West, second Lord Sackville (1827–1908). Reclusive in his later years, the second Lord Sackville suffered from what Sackville-West once called 'the temperamental melancholy which dogs all Sackvilles and has driven many of them to end their lives in blackest solitude', and he spent most of his time withdrawn in his study.[4]

Nevertheless, he enjoyed the company of children.[5] Sackville-West later recalled how, wrapped in a Shetland shawl by his nanny, who 'mistrusted the draughts in that endless house', he took his great-uncle's hand to tour his future inheritance: 'And so we went – very slowly indeed, for he was old and I was not yet at all firm on my legs – in and out of the dim old rooms and passages, up and down stairs (one step at a time) and along what seemed miles of gallery, with the peak of the shawl trailing far out on the floor behind me.'[6] They would look together at the 'shadowy interior of a huge Caroline four-poster bed hung with crimson silk, or a tall Meissen vase painted with a design of red chrysanthemums'. The young Sackville-West was occasionally allowed to touch these mysterious and precious objects, 'repeating aloud as I did so the lesson learnt from Nanny: "Great Uncle Lionel's things are very precious and I must be very careful not to break them."'[7]

Lord Sackville shared Knole with his daughter Victoria (1862–1936), her husband and cousin Lionel (1867–1928), who became third Lord Sackville in 1908, and their daughter, Vita.[8] Sackville-West's evolving sensibility for Knole was intertwined with his relationship with Vita, who was 10 years his senior. Although he described their friendship as 'one of the most intimate and enduring' of his life, the issue of inheritance would always be divisive.[9] Vita was notoriously territorial about Knole as a child and not at all keen on visits made to the house by other children.[10] She later confided to her husband, Harold Nicolson (1886–1968), 'I used to hate Eddy when he was a baby…because he would have Knole.'[11] In contrast to Vita, Sackville-West was a frail and sickly child, having inherited telangiectasia from his mother, which meant that he suffered from frequent nosebleeds.[12] Vita observed him 'passing from critical illness to critical illness' and on better days being carried downstairs in his enormous shawl to play the piano, 'his puny little legs dangling, as unable to touch the pedals as his tiny hands were to span an octave'.[13] Vita's inability to inherit Knole due to her gender and Sackville-West's failure to love the house in the same way that she did has meant that he has often been cast as an obstructive, reluctant heir.

The diarist James Lees-Milne (1908–97), who knew them both, observed the 'strange emotional duet' that played out between the two as adults: 'Vita resented the fact that she had been born a girl, whereas Eddy may have regretted being born a boy. Vita loved Knole with such an atavistic passion that it was a torture of the psyche that she would never own it. Eddy who was not brought up there as a child was bored by Knole and dreaded the responsibility of ownership and burden.'[14] This tension was subtly expressed in their respective writing: Vita published her authoritative history, *Knole and the Sackvilles*, in 1922, while Sackville-West cast Knole as Vair in his claustrophobic 1926 gothic novel *The Ruin*.[15] Interestingly, both referred to the weight their aristocratic legacy placed on their shoulders. Vita rather pointedly remarked on their descent from 'a race too prodigal, too amorous, too weak, too indolent, and too melancholy' in her personal dedication to Sackville-West in his copy of *Knole and the Sackvilles*.[16] In *The Ruin*, Sackville-West alluded to the overbearing 'mystical law of the house, which bade the keepers of its treasures utter the essential feelings of its own stage. The pictures – the countless pictures – the china, the carving, the silver, the gold, the furniture – all possessed a composite soul with which to rule their masters.'[17]

The rivalry between Sackville-West and Vita extended to their respective encounters with the artists, writers and intellectuals that made up the Bloomsbury Group – especially the novelist Virginia Woolf (1882–1941), with whom Vita had a well-documented affair. Sackville-West first encountered the Bloomsbury Group at Garsington Manor near Oxford, the home of society hostess Lady Ottoline Morrell, whom he had met through her nephew Lord Morven Cavendish-Bentinck.[18] At Eton together, they were among a group of young aesthetes, Sackville-West was particularly celebrated for his talent at the piano, performing Chopin and Debussy at school concerts.[19] By 1922, he was part of a circle of striking, sharp and literary Oxford undergraduates visiting Garsington that included Raymond Mortimer (1895–1980), Lord David Cecil (1902–86) and L.P. Hartley (1895–1972). At Garsington they mixed with established cultural figures, such as the poets Siegfried Sassoon and T.S. Eliot and the novelist E.M. Forster. The writer Rosamond Lehmann found Sackville-West to be 'a perfectly *awful* character, saved only by his glorious capacity for jokes and laughter'.[20]

Morrell photographed Sackville-West's first meeting with Woolf and Lytton Strachey on 3 June 1923 (Fig. 4), and Woolf wrote to T.S. Eliot the next day to report sitting at dinner with 'a young Lord at Oxford who said Mr Eliot was his favourite poet'.[21] 'I like them all (especially Mrs Woolf) but I mistrust their minds fundamentally,' Sackville-West wrote a year later to Vita, frustrated by

4

5

FIG 4 *Lord David Cecil, Edward Sackville-West, 5th Baron Sackville, Virginia Woolf and Lytton Strachey*, 1923, Lady Ottoline Morrell (1873–1938), photographic print, 9.1 x 6cm, National Portrait Gallery, London

FIG 5 *The Apology of Arthur Rimbaud by Edward Sackville-West*, published by Hogarth Press in 1927, with a board binding designed by Vanessa Bell (1879–1961), paper and board, 17 x 10.8 x 1.2cm, Knole, Kent (Sackville Collection) Photo: the author

their apparent inability to commit themselves to fixed viewpoints.[22] Although an outwardly warm friendship was established between Woolf and Sackville-West – she published his essay *The Apology of Arthur Rimbaud* through the Hogarth Press in 1927 (Fig. 5) and offered him hospitality at her home, Monk's House, in Rodmell, East Sussex – she could be waspish about him in private correspondence.[23] In January 1925, she informed the painter Jacques Raverat that a 'tiny lap dog, called Sackville-West, came to see me the other day (a cousin of my aristocrat and will inherit Knole) and my cook said Who was the lady in the Drawing room? He has a voice like a girl's, and a face like a Persian cat's, all white and serious, with large violet eyes and fluffy cheeks.'[24]

6

Despite being intrigued by the aristocracy, part of Woolf's objection to Sackville-West and some of his friends was their inclination to 'paint and powder which wasn't the style in our day'.[25] Although members of the Bloomsbury Group were open to new relationships with both sexes while in established partnerships and marriages, some initially disapproved of the emerging taste for flamboyant dress and camp manners that they observed in the younger generation. Frances Partridge (neé Marshall), a great friend of Sackville-West, described him as being among the 'host of quite young fringe-Bloomsburies' – a group that included Mortimer and the sculptor Stephen Tomlin, with whom Sackville-West had a turbulent romantic relationship and who created a portrait bust of him. They met at the Charlotte Street studio of the painter Duncan Grant (1885–1978), partner of Woolf's sister, Vanessa Bell. Mortimer, Grant and Tomlin formed the Cranium Club on 23 January 1923 and Sackville-West was invited along 'for conversation and the exchange of ideas'.[26] In the era of the Bright Young Things, this group met for parties at Charlotte Street, at which profound talk slowly receded as nights wore on, to be replaced by 'casual lovemaking and energetic dancing' to a soundtrack of the Blues or Charleston, and the guests 'let off steam, sexual and otherwise'.[27] Particularly notorious was a 'hermaphrodite party' hosted by Sackville-West and Nancy Morris (girlfriend of Sackville-West's close confidant, the psychoanalyst Alix Strachey), at which 'most of the young men had loaded themselves with pearls and paint; the atmosphere was stifling and the noise so defeaning that even the music from a vast gramophone horn was inaudible.'[28]

The rich cultural atmosphere of Sackville-West's circle influenced his aesthetic taste, as expressed in the decoration of his apartment in the Gatehouse Tower and West Range at Knole. These rooms were given to him by the third Lord Sackville in 1926. In January of that year Vita described 'Eddy chattering' about paint colours for his new rooms in a letter to Woolf and asking 'Shall I have my sitting room pink or yellow[?].'[29] He is likely to have received advice on decoration and fittings from the architect Paul Geddes Hyslop, later the partner of Mortimer, who was also a close friend and made an annual visit to see Sackville-West at Knole, often at Christmas.[30] 'Mr Edward's Rooms' were located along the first floor of West Range as well as in the Gatehouse Tower. They were served by a kitchen and his housekeeper's rooms below and were characterised by brightly coloured interior paintwork throughout. The rooms were accessed from Green Court via a staircase painted sage green. This colour continued on the landing and the walls and joinery of the dining room and bathroom on the first floor, where there were also two guest bedrooms, one painted dark blue, the other mustard. A lobby of green connected these to the stone spiral staircase of the Gatehouse Tower, lit by a wrought-iron cage lantern, which led up to Sackville-West's bedroom and the music room. His bedroom walls were painted stone white, with floor-height fitted bookshelves in stippled blue built to accommodate his vast library. The doors, curtain pelmets and windowsills were also painted blue with mouldings picked out in peach, while a further three small turret rooms housed a white dressing room, a red bathroom and a blue toilet, all of which were separated from the main room by a full-length red curtain at each door.[31] Above, the music room's walls were painted bright pink. The room was fitted with large bookshelves, pelmets and a picture rail painted dark blue. In each of the turrets, the walls were painted in contrasting colours of charcoal, blue and green. One of the turrets became known as the 'Nietzsche Room' and was decorated with graffiti of pseudo-runes, symbols of the zodiac and part of a musical score. It is possible that a life-size sketch in charcoal of a male figure and a dog drawn directly on to the plaster of the music room, which has recently been revealed beneath later paint layers, is a portrait of Sackville-West by either Grant or the artist John Banting (1902–72), both of whom stayed in the Gatehouse Tower and contributed to the decoration.

Paul Geddes Hyslop was among Sackville-West's first guests at Knole, staying there from 21 to 26 May 1926, coinciding with Vita, who came to dine at Knole on 23 May. She returned home to Long Barn to write a horrified account of Sackville-West's rooms to her husband, who was then serving as a chargé d'affaires for the British Diplomatic Service in Tehran:

I dined at Knole, and there was Eddy, with Paul Heslop [sic]. Darling, his rooms are rather awful. He has a pale mauve light in his bedroom. Then the three stone turret rooms at the three corners of his sitting room are eingerichtet with a sort of ninety-ish affectation, – a green light in one, a red light in another, a yellow light in the third; a rapier propped up in the corner, a crucifix on the wall. It made me cross; it was all so decadent, theatrical, and cheap. My lovely Knole! And

Eddy himself mincing in black velvet. I didn't dislike Paul Heslop, but the whole establishment had a nasty flavour about it. I don't object to homosexuality, but I do hate decadence. And it is a nasty fungoid growth on Knole of all places.[32]

Vita's objection centred, like Woolf's earlier comments on Sackville-West's appearance, on his particular personal aesthetic, characterised by both as 'decadence'. This was a term in common use in the 1920s and 1930s, applied by the press in a derogatory way to the emerging generation of cultured, flamboyant, often homosexual young men such as the socialites Stephen Tennant and Edward Gaythorne-Hardy, who were both members of Sackville-West's wider social circle.[33] Some of the interior arrangements that Vita described were recorded on the first bookplate produced for Sackville-West at Knole (Fig. 6). Gothic in style, and inspired by *Saint Jerome in his Study*, a 1514 engraving by Albrecht Dürer, a copy of which Sackville-West owned, it shows his desk adorned with quills, a candlestick, an hourglass and a skull with a row of books, including his recently published first novel, *Piano Quintet* (1925). The Sackville arms decorate a shield on the wall above and the breeze from the open window gently moves the curtains and disturbs loose sheet music. Lytton Strachey visited Sackville-West on 28 August and shared some of Vita's misgivings about his personal style: 'Knole was interesting – beautiful on the whole externally, with College-like courts and charming gardens and park, but the inside was disappointing – too much-hole and-corner Elizabethanism; one longed for the spaciousness of the 18th century; and the bad taste of countless generations of Sackvilles littered it all up. Eddy, it seemed to me, continued this tradition in his ladylike apartments.'[34]

Sackville-West filled his rooms with furniture plundered from the vast collection of 'Knole Heirlooms': the 1928 Knole inventory lists large amounts of satinwood and mahogany furniture and three pieces of Brussels tapestry.[35] These sat alongside a large E.M.G. gramophone and a 1926 Steinway baby grand piano. Sackville-West also surrounded himself with a large collection of 'books, gramophone records and bibelots'.[36] These he combined with screens and cupboards painted by contemporary artists. Duncan Grant, with whom, by 1926, he was having an affair, stayed with him at Knole between 3 and 5 July and again between 11 and 13 December and painted a fire screen for the music room of swirling blue and green flames framed by curtains that contrasted with the pink walls (Fig. 7). Next to it, Sackville-West later hung a series of his sketch studies of male nudes.[37] Grant's portrait of Sackville-West painted during this period shows him seated in concentration at the piano against a background of chintz wallpaper (Fig. 8). Grant's daughter Angelica Garnett recalled listening as a child to Sackville-West playing an 'old square piano…very charmingly' during one visit to Charleston.[38]

Another artist with whom Sackville-West was to share an intense relationship was the surrealist painter John Banting, who made nine visits to Knole between February and September 1927, staying for two weeks in August of

7

FIG 7 Fire screen, *c.* 1926,
Duncan Grant (1885–1978),
oil on paper laid on canvas,
124.5 x 147.3cm, Knole, Kent
(Sackville Collection)
Photo: © Christie's Ltd
© Estate of Duncan Grant.

FIG 8 *Edward Sackville-West,*
c. 1927–28, Duncan Grant, oil
on canvas, 75.5 x 64.8cm, Knole,
Kent (Sackville Collection)
Photo: Ben Blossom, 2016
© Estate of Duncan Grant.

8

FIG 9 *John Banting*, *c.* 1927–28, artist unknown, photographic print on paper, 18 x 12cm, Knole, Kent (Sackville Collection) Photo: Richard Holttum, 2016

FIG 10 Photograph of John Banting (1902–72) painting a corner cupboard at Knole, *c.* 1927, Edward Sackville-West (1901–65), private collection Photo: Ben Blossom, 2016

9

10

that year. The men are likely to have met through Grant, as Banting kept a studio in Fitzroy Street, London, from 1925, which brought him into contact with Bloomsbury Group painters.[39] Sackville-West sat for a portrait by him that year.[40] Considered by the artist and poet John Trevelyan to be an 'eternal outsider', Banting was nevertheless a handsome and glamorous figure in the 1920s, as at home in Paris as he was in London.[41] Sackville-West found him 'congenial, interesting, good + beautiful', though later believed his preoccupation with drinking and sex prevented him from realising his full talent.[42] Their time together at Knole is recorded in a series of photographs that survive in the personal albums of both men.[43] Sackville-West was captured humorously addressing the skull from his desk or reclining like a statue on a plinth in the Orangery, where Banting later posed for a more studied portrait (Fig. 9). Banting photographed montages of paper, photographs or objects in semi-abstract arrangements, and reworked Sackville-West's Gatehouse Tower bookplate into a contemporary design (Fig. 11).[44] He also took one of the few known pictures of Sackville-West in the Gatehouse Tower. In it, Sackville-West appears in the music room, sitting in a 'Charles II winged easy chair' next to a large vase of lilies, with his library of books behind him. While at Knole, Banting also painted the box of Sackville-West's E.M.G. gramophone and three pieces of furniture. One was a four-fold screen (now in a private collection) featuring large, stylised figures representing the arts, a diver plunging into a lake below a church and a male torso on a plinth. The second was a corner cupboard (still at Knole) decorated with nude figures and urns among flowers that may have been inspired by the gardens at Knole (Fig. 10). The third was a wardrobe (likewise still at Knole) with flower motifs on a black ground. The cupboard includes a tiny monochrome portrait of the artist holding a brush. It is comparable to the decoration Banting undertook for Ralph Partridge and Frances Marshall at Ham Spray, which included tiny portraits of their friends, among them studies of Sackville-West and Mortimer, who were known affectionately as the 'little friends'.[45] Through Banting, Sackville-West is likely to have met the photographer Barbara Ker-Seymer, who photographed him against the backdrop of charging horses painted by Banting that decorated the walls of her studio above the jeweller Asprey on New Bond Street (Fig. 1).

During the late 1920s and early 1930s, Sackville-West entertained a steady stream of visitors. They included the novelist Aldous Huxley, who had been his tutor at Eton, Desmond MacCarthy, editor of the *New Statesman*, of which Sackville-West became the music critic in 1935, and the composer Ethel Smyth. More glamorous figures included the society photographer Cecil Beaton and the film star Anna May Wong. Vita, in a letter to Virginia Woolf, described a party at Knole on 29 May 1927 'attended by slim young creatures all looking as though they had come straight out of *The Tatler*, all indistinguishable one from another, and the young men to match. They lay about on the grass, like aristocratic young animals with sleek heads.'[46] Sackville-West also left Knole for long periods, for example spending the summer of 1930 with

Mortimer and staying with the Huxleys at their villa in Sanary (where he wrote part of *Simpson*, the story of a nanny in service, which became his most acclaimed and popular novel).[47] Close friends, Sackville-West, Mortimer and Huxley each commissioned a portrait bust from the Berlin sculptor Paul Hamann between 1929 and 1930 (they are now in the collection of the National Portrait Gallery).[48] Fortuitously, Sackville-West's life mask has survived, mounted onto the wall of the spiral staircase outside the music room (Fig. 14). This is likely to be the one created by Hamann, from which he later made the bust.[49] Cast in plaster, with the eyes directed downwards and each eyelash clearly rendered, it conveys a surreal presence.

The burden of Sackville-West's inheritance was ever present. His father became fourth Lord Sackville in 1928, the year Woolf immortalised both Vita and Knole in her novel *Orlando*. The combined financial burden of tax and maintenance prompted the sale of furniture and paintings from the house.[50] By 1936, negotiations to pass Knole to the National Trust were underway, overseen by James Lees-Milne, secretary of the Country Houses Committee, who had stayed with Sackville-West in the Gatehouse Tower. He recalled the lengthy negotiations, during which 'Eddy's obstructive unborn sons became a sick joke.' Interrupted by the Second World War, they were finally concluded in 1946.[51] By then, Sackville-West had already left Knole. He was ill and depressed, in part due to the conflict, and was described by Woolf as being left with a 'face tossed up from the bottom of the sea'. He was saved from suicide by the intervention of E.M. Forster.[52] The last entries in his visitors' book are those for Mortimer, the music critic Desmond Shawe-Taylor (1907–95) and Eardley Knollys (1902–91), a painter and art dealer.[53] After leaving Knole, Sackville-West went first to Upton, the house of Sir Kenneth Clark, director of the National Gallery, and then to West Wycombe Park, where he was to see out the war. He finally settled at Long Crichel in Dorset, together with Mortimer, Shawe-Taylor and Knollys. Sackville-West marked his departure from Knole by commissioning two views of the building from John Piper. One was of the house from the north, showing the architectural expanse of the building combining multiple grey towers and gables with great stretches of red roofs and chimneys beneath a characteristically dark and brooding sky. The other was of the inner Gatehouse Tower, in which the solidity of the great walls is rendered in a range of greys and ochres, filling the canvas (Fig. 15). Thanking Piper on receipt of the pictures on 16 February 1943, Sackville-West wrote:

the oils arrived today & I am delighted with them. The one of the House Front seems to me indeed one of the best things of yours I have seen. Above all it is so very different from all your other oils: the palette seems more extensive & the sky especially magnificent. I really am most grateful to you for taking so much trouble, as I foresee that in future these pictures are all that will remain to me of Knole.[54]

During the war, Sackville-West worked as a radio producer and broadcaster for the BBC's Third Programme, also volunteering for the Red Cross, where he become friends with Jane Phillips (1919–99), who fell in love with him, though the feeling was never requited. 'It was just one of those things that happen to one,' she later observed.[55] In 1953, having visited an exhibition of Graham Sutherland's work at the Tate Gallery, she and her husband, Ian Phillips, commissioned the artist to paint Sackville-West's portrait, which was started in November of that year.[56] Sackville-West was both a friend and patron of Sutherland, publishing a monograph on the artist in 1943 that included works from his own collection. He invited the Sutherlands to Knole in 1939 and again in 1943, on which occasion they

11

presented him with a copy of *Poems 1937–1942* by David Gascoyne, which Sutherland had illustrated (Fig. 12). On 6 March 1955, Partridge accompanied an enthusiastic Sackville-West to Somerset to see his newly completed portrait: 'The portrait is a remarkable work and has a considerable likeness to Eddy, but there is something definitely unpleasant about it – whether its tints of mauve and lime green, or that it seems to depict him in his electric chair waiting for his quietus' (Fig. 13). Sackville-West wrote to Sutherland two days later to congratulate him:

I must say I think it absolutely masterly…It is the face I see when I look in the glass, but the expression is very different. I always expected you to find me out & of course you have. The picture is the portrait of a very frightened man – almost a ghost, for nothing is solid except the face and hands. All my life I have been afraid of things – other people, loud noises, what may be going to happen next – of life in fact. This is what you have shown…I am profoundly impressed. I am quite sure it is a work of genius, which will continue to interest people long after I have been forgotten.[57]

Vita was more succinct in her observation, quipping 'It's Eddy to the death.'[58]

In 1956 Sackville-West bought Cooleville in County Tipperary, close to the home in Kildorrery of his friend the novelist Elizabeth Bowen, with whom he had often stayed. He was attracted by the Irish climate and the warmth and friendliness of the inhabitants.[59] The following year he gave up his interest in Knole in favour of his nephew Lionel Sackville-West

FIG 11 Reworking of Edward Sackville-West's *Ex Libris* bookplate, *c.* 1927, John Banting, paper, 10.1 x 7.6cm, Knole, Kent (Sackville Collection) Photo: Richard Holttum, 2016 © John Banting (1902–72)/ Bridgeman Images 2016

FIG 12 *Poems 1937–42*, 1943, David Gascoyne (1916–2001), illustrated by Graham Sutherland (1903–80) and inscribed 'Eddy with love from Graham & Katharine Christmas 1943', paper and board, 21.5 x 16.8 x 1.2cm, Knole, Kent (Sackville Collection) Photo: Richard Holttum, 2016 © The Estate of Graham Sutherland

12

13

FIG 13 *Edward Sackville-West*,
1955, Graham Sutherland, oil
and gouache on canvas, 165.5 x
77.3cm, Knole, Kent
Photo: Ben Blossom, 2016
© The Estate of Graham
Sutherland

(1913–2004), explaining in an interview, 'Ireland suits my temperament. I prefer it to that big place in Kent and I love this house – where I can write books, review classical records, and play my grand piano … here I can farm a few acres and entertain a few friends. That is all I ask from life.'[60] Despite inheriting the Sackville barony from his father in 1962, becoming fifth Lord Sackville, he told Leonard Woolf two years later:

> Living at Knole now is (to me, at any rate) extremely disagreeable – particularly in summer, when it is all but impossible to walk outside the garden walls without stepping on a prone figure. It is like living in the middle of Hyde Park! However my cousin Lionel luckily loves the house enough to put up with this (and other) features of the modern world, none of which I can abide.[61]

Sackville-West died at Cooleville on 4 July 1965. When news of his death reached Nancy Mitford in Venice, she exclaimed in a letter to her sister Deborah Cavendish, Duchess of Devonshire, 'Eddy! I'm shattered. Had no idea…Graham Sutherland said what a pretty shawl you've got on – I said Eddy gave it to me – he said Eddy who's dead? DEAD? I nearly fainted…oh dear, I mind Monsewer.'[62] A Catholic convert, Sackville-West chose to be buried at St Mary's Church, Clogheen, rather than in the Sackville family crypt at Withyham.[63]

Sutherland's portrait of Edward Sackville-West was bequeathed to the National Trust by Jane Phillips. It will go on permanent display in the Gatehouse Tower, Knole, in June 2016.

Emma Slocombe is the National Trust's Curator for Knole, Kent.

ACKNOWLEDGEMENTS
I am most grateful to Lord and Lady Sackville for permission to study the private collection and archive at Knole and for placing significant items on loan to the National Trust for display in the Gatehouse Tower and to the Hon. Mrs Hugh (Bridget) Sackville-West for her generous support throughout my research into the life of Edward Sackville-West at Knole. I am also grateful to Helen Fawbert, Vicky Patient and Roo Gunzy for their invaluable assistance and the provision of information.

1. For the history of the Gatehouse Tower, see National Trust Archives (henceforth NTA), Elizabeth Jamieson & Peter Kidd, 'A Survey of the Documentary and Visual Evidence Relating to the former appearance and use of the West Range and Gatehouse Tower at Knole', 2012.
2. See Michael De-la-Noy, *Eddy: The Life of Edward Sackville-West*, London, 1988, pp. 1–2. Major Charles John Sackville-West (1870–1962), who became fourth Lord Sackville in 1928, was the second son of Lieutenant-Colonel the Hon. William Sackville-West (1830–1905), who was himself the sixth son of George West, fifth Earl De La Warr (1791–1869), whose descendants inherited Knole as a result of his marriage to Lady Elizabeth Sackville, Baroness Buckhurst (d. 1870), the daughter of John Fredrick Sackville, third Duke of Dorset (1745–99).
3. H. Avray Tipping, 'Bourne Park, Kent, part I', *Country Life*, 6 May 1922, pp. 602–09; H. Avray Tipping, 'Bourne Park, Kent, part II', *Country Life*, 13 May 1922, pp. 636–44.
4. Robert Sackville-West, *Inheritance: The Story of Knole and the Sackvilles*, London, 2010, p. 187.
5. Vita Sackville-West 'Part One', Nigel Nicolson (ed.), *Portrait of a Marriage*, London, 1973, pp. 12–13.
6. De-la-Noy, op. cit., pp. 5–6.
7. Ibid, pp. 7–8.
8. Victoria was the second child of Lionel Sackville-West, second Lord Sackville (1827–1908) and Josefa Duran (1830–71), a dancer known as Pepita. See Sackville-West, *Inheritance*, op. cit., pp. 172–73.
9. Ibid, p. 187.
10. Victoria Glendinning, *Vita: The Life of V. Sackville-West*, London, 1983, p. 14.
11. Vita Sackville-West to Harold Nicolson, 4 July 1912, quoted in Nigel

Nicolson (ed.), *Vita & Harold: The Letters of Vita Sackville-West & Harold Nicolson 1910–1962*, London, 1992, p. 97.

12. De-la-Noy, op. cit., p. 17.

13. Nicolson (ed.), *Portrait of a Marriage*, op. cit., pp. 12–13.

14. James Lees-Milne, *People and Places: Country House Donors and the National Trust*, London, 1992, p. 168.

15. Vair in heraldic terms references the blue and white geometric pattern on the Sackville arms. With thanks to Vicky Patient for this information.

16. Vita Sackville-West, *Knole and the Sackvilles*, London, 1922, p. 29. The full dedication reads, 'E. Sackville-West from V. Sackville-West, Christmas 1922 "of a race too prodigal, too amorous, too weak, too indolent, and too melancholy." p. 29.' (private collection).

17. Edward Sackville-West, *The Ruin*, London, 1926, p. 139.

18. Michael De-la-Noy, 'Edward Sackville-West', *Charleston Magazine*, issue VIII, 1993, p. 22

19. De-la-Noy, *Eddy*, op. cit., pp. 14–17.

20. Selina Hastings, *Rosamond Lehmann: A Life*, London, 2002.

21. Nigel Nicolson (ed.), *A Change of Perspective: The Letters of Virginia Woolf 1923–1928*, London, 1977, p. 45.

22. Ibid., p. 23.

23. Private collection, 'E S-W 1922–1929' (photograph album).

24. Virginia Woolf writing to Jacques Raverat, 24 January 1925, in Nicolson (ed.), *A Change of Perspective*, op. cit., pp. 154–55.

25. Ibid.

26. Knole, Sackville Collection (henceforth SC), 'Invitation to join the Cranium Club', 23 January 1925.

27. Frances Partridge, *Love in Bloomsbury: Memories*, London, 1981, pp. 90–91.

28. Ibid., p. 178

29. Victoria Glendinning, *Vita: The Life of V. Sackville-West*, London, 1983, p. 151.

30. The painted decoration of the drawing room at Long Crichel undertaken in the 1940s matches that of Eddy's bedroom in the Gatehouse Tower at Knole.

31. For the decorative history of the Gatehouse Tower, see NTA, James Finlay, 'Knole: Eddy's Rooms in the Gatehouse Tower', January 2014 & November 2015 and NTA, Lisa Oestriecher, 'Inspired by Knole: Paint Research Report', November 2014.

32. Indiana University Library, Sackville-West, V. mss, correspondence, Box 2: 1919, July–1926, June.

33. D.J. Taylor, *Bright Young People*, London, 2007, pp. 204–205.

34. De-la-Noy, *Eddy*, op. cit., p. 111.

35. SC, 'Inventory of Furniture at Knole, 1928'. Sackville-West took some of these pieces to Long Crichel, Dorset, in 1953 and then to Cooleville, Ireland. They returned to Knole following his death.

36. Frances Partridge, *Everything to Lose: Diaries 1945–1960*, London, 1985, p. 289. E.M.G. Hand-Made Gramophones Ltd was founded by Ellis Michael Ginn in 1923. Sackville-West's model at Knole was an E.M.G. Mark X.

37. Mary Bates, secretary to conductor Malcolm Sargent (1895–1967) who occupied the Gatehouse Tower during the Second World War, in conversation with the author at Knole, 2015.

38. De-la-Noy, 'Edward Sackville-West', op. cit., p. 23.

39. Jane Stevenson, *Edward Burra: Twentieth-Century Eye*, London, 2007, p. 112.

40. De-la-Noy, *Eddy*, op. cit., p. 100.

41. Ibid.

42. Taylor, op. cit., p. 204.

43. Tate Gallery Archives (henceforth TGA), 779/8/373; Private collection, Photograph album of Edward Sackville-West, c. 1926–80.

44. TGA, 779/8/373, p. 32.

45. Partridge, *Love in Bloomsbury*, op. cit., p. 158.

46. De-la-Noy, *Eddy*, op. cit., pp. 114–115.

47. Sybille Bedford, *Aldous Huxley: A Biography Volume 1, 1894–1939*, London, 1973, pp. 256–57.

48. National Portrait Gallery (hereafter NPG) 6071, Edward Sackville-West by Paul Hamann, Plaster, 1929; NPG 5403, Aldous Huxley by Paul Hamann, Bronze, 1930; NPG 6070, Raymond Mortimer by Paul Hamann, Plaster, 1930.

49. Harold Nicolson also had a life mask made in Berlin in 1929. See De-la-Noy, *Eddy*, op. cit., p. 109.

50. Elsewhere in this issue, John Chu discusses the acquisition of the portrait of Louis-Pierre Quentin de Richebourg, marquis de Champcenetz, by Thomas Gainsborough in 2016, one of the pictures sold by Sackville-West's father, Charles, fourth Lord Sackville, in 1930. See De-la-Noy, *Eddy*, op. cit., pp. 150–51.

51. James Lees-Milne, op. cit., p. 170.

52. De-la-Noy, *Eddy*, op. cit., p. 179. Virginia Woolf described meeting Sackville-West 'and he really wrung my heart – like a face tossed up from the bottom of the sea' in a letter to Vita on 19 August 1939.

53. Eardley Knollys owned the Storran Gallery at 106 Brompton Road, London, in the 1930s with Frank Coombs, showing the work of British artists, such as Duncan Grant and John Banting, and French and Italian artists, such as Pablo Picasso and Amedeo Modigliani. See Frances Partridge, 'Edward Eardley Knollys', *Charleston Magazine*, issue V, reprinted in *Eardley Knollys 1902–1991: Selected works from The Studio Estate*, London, 2014, p. 21.

54. TGA, 200410/1/1/3327.

55. 'Jane Phillips', *The Guardian*, 6 August 1999.

56. Ibid.

57. De-la-Noy, *Eddy*, op. cit., p. 271. Sutherland completed a second half-length portrait of Sackville-West in 1957. It was sold by the artist to Birmingham Museum and Art Gallery the following year.

58. Ibid, p. 272.

59. Ibid, pp. 279–81.

60. 'Baron's son gives up the stately home for a quiet life in the country', *Daily Mail*, 28 August 1958

61. De-la-Noy, *Eddy*, op. cit., p. 304

62. Ibid, p. 309–10.

63. Ibid, p. 311.

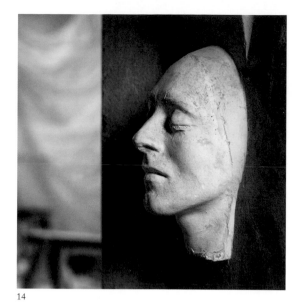

14

FIG 14 Life mask cast in plaster of Edward Sackville-West, c. 1929–30, attrib. to Paul Hamann (1891–1973)
Photo: Ben Blossom, 2016

FIG 15 *The Gatehouse, Knole*, 1942, John Piper (1903–92), oil on canvas laid over board, 63.5 x 76.2cm
Photo: Offer Waterman, London
© The Piper Estate/DACS 2016

1

A GALLERY OF FAME
THE EVIDENCE FOR A JACOBEAN
PORTRAIT FRIEZE AT KNOLE

The bust portraits in the Brown Gallery are of a uniform shape and size and have distinctive wooden frames. CATHERINE DAUNT examines the evidence that the paintings were commissioned as a set in the early 17th century and originally hung as a portrait frieze in the Cartoon Gallery

AMONG THE MANY PAINTINGS in the collection at Knole
is a set of 44 bust portraits primarily depicting famous
figures from the 16th century.[1] Currently hanging in the
Brown Gallery on the first floor (Fig. 1), the paintings
in this set can be distinguished from others in the room
by their distinctive framing devices. Each portrait is set
within a feigned oval outlined in brown-red paint and
defined by boldly gilded spandrels, which are decorated
with a stencilled vine-leaf design, also painted in brown-
red. In addition, they all have gilded wooden frames with
egg-and-dart mouldings and carved wooden ribbons,
which are nailed to the top sections of the frames and
overhang the pictures. Also gilded, each of these ribbons
is painted with the name and title of the figure depicted.
With the exception of a single example on canvas (depicting James VI and I), these portraits are all painted on
wooden panels measuring around 80 x 63.5cm. The set
was recorded in its current location in 18th-century
inventories, but until recently little was known about its
origins. As the result of new research, however, it is now
possible to argue with confidence that the majority of
these portraits were produced in the early years of the 17th
century as a single commission. Furthermore, a recent
discovery in the long gallery, now known as the Cartoon
Gallery, strongly indicates that the set was originally made
to hang as a portrait frieze beneath the cornice in this
room. It is highly likely, therefore, that the set was made
specifically for Knole and that it was commissioned by
Thomas Sackville, first Earl of Dorset (1536–1608), as
part of his extensive remodelling of the house between
1605 and 1608. This article presents the evidence for this
and considers both the original method of display and the
probable function of the set.

The Date of the Set

The paintings in this set have hitherto been difficult to
date with accuracy due to a lack of documentary evidence
and various restorations that have left most extensively
overpainted. Also clearly the result of a later intervention,
the decorative spandrels and carved ribbons have made
it difficult to ascertain whether or not the current set was
produced *en bloc* or collected over time. Prior to the new
research, the set had been tentatively dated to around
1600, largely due to the identities of the figures depicted.[2]
However, as a result of a dendrochronological survey carried out on 22 of the panels, it is now possible to provide a
more accurate date for the set.[3] Combined with a detailed
visual examination of the rest of the paintings, the study
strongly indicates that 38 of the portraits in the group
were produced as a single commission in 1607–08. The
close examination of the paintings and, in particular, their
supports, also provides evidence that six of the portraits in
the current group were added to the set at a later date.

The oak panels used for the 38 core paintings were all
constructed in a very similar way, notably using tongue-
and-groove joints to connect the individual boards. In
addition, all but one of the panels analysed contains wood
from a tree that was also used to make at least one other
panel in the set. For example, the panels used for the

portraits of Bishop Stephen Gardiner, William of Orange,
Henry Howard, Earl of Northampton and Francis, Duke
of Guise, were all found to contain wood from a common tree. Other individual trees were also identified
across several panels within the set. These strong physical
connections make it very likely that all 38 panels were
produced together. On this basis, the dendrochronology provides a *terminus post quem* for the set. The most
recent tree identified cannot have been felled any earlier
than 1605, so the set must have been produced after this
date.[4] If the tree was felled in 1605 or 1606, however, it is
entirely plausible that the panels could have been made
in 1607 or 1608.

An examination of the figures represented provides
further evidence that the set was produced around this
time. Apart from two medieval figures, Roger Bacon
(*c.* 1214–92) and John Wyclif (d. 1384), all of the people
depicted were alive in the 16th century and they had all
achieved fame by the time the first Earl of Dorset died
in 1608.[5] The sitters include English statesmen, courtiers,
prelates, soldiers and adventurers, plus a group of eight
foreign military leaders with whom the English had
contact during the Tudor period or in the early years of
James's reign. The choice of sitters points to a date for
the set that corresponds with the dendrochronology. The
inclusion of Richard Bancroft, for example, suggests that
the set was produced after 1604, when Bancroft became
Archbishop of Canterbury. The fact that no later archbishops are represented may indicate that the set was produced
before Bancroft died in 1610 (although it is possible that
some of the original portraits have been lost). Furthermore, the portrait of Robert Cecil, first Earl of Salisbury,
may provide evidence that the set was produced in 1606
or later. Based on a portrait type developed by John de
Critz the Elder (d. 1642) in around 1602, the composition shows Salisbury wearing a blue ribbon around his
neck, from which the Lesser George would presumably
have been suspended (the insignia itself is not visible). As
Salisbury was only made a Knight of the Garter in 1606, it
is probable that the painting dates from this year or later.

The Later Additions

Of the 22 panels that were analysed using dendrochronology, only one was found to have no physical connection to
the others in the set. The portrait of a figure identified by
the inscription on the wooden ribbon as 'Admiral Blake'
is one of six that were almost certainly added to the set
in the late 18th century (Fig. 2). The panel used for this
painting, which was constructed using butt joints rather
than tongue-and-groove joints, was found to contain
wood from a tree that cannot have been felled before
1610, which indicates that it was constructed at a slightly
later date than the rest of the set. It is the only painting
in the set with a background view (a naval scene) and the
only one containing a coat of arms. Furthermore, chipped
paint along the bottom edge indicates that it has probably
been cut down from a larger composition.[6] The inscription
on the ribbon presumably refers to the famous English
admiral Robert Blake (*c.* 1598–1657), although as Charles

FIG 2 A Commander, previously misidentified as Admiral Lord Blake, 1600–29, British School, oil on oak panel, 69 x 54.3cm, Knole, Kent
Photo: Ben Blossom, 2016

FIG 3 *Queen Elizabeth I*, 1600–29/1793, British School, oil on oak panel with repainted and re-embellished frame, 69 x 54.3cm, Knole, Kent
Photo: Ben Blossom, 2016

J. Phillips noted in 1929, the costume appears to be too early for this identification to be reliable.[7] The coat of arms has been associated with the Fenner (or Venour) family and it has therefore been suggested that the sitter could have been Captain George Fenner (*c.* 1540–1618), but this has not been confirmed and the provenance of the painting remains unknown.[8]

None of the other five paintings identified as later additions were suitable for dendrochronology, but there is enough evidence from elsewhere to disassociate them from the original set. The portrait of James VI and I is based on a face type developed in or after 1616 by Paul van Somer (*c.* 1576–1621), making it too late to be part of the original group. The only other monarchs represented in the set are Henry VIII, Mary I and Elizabeth I (Fig. 3), but the portraits of these figures, too, have been identified as later additions. Although on panel, each of these paintings has been enlarged on all sides with additional sections of wood, over which the painting has been extended (Fig. 4). It is possible that the central sections, which appear to be from the 17th century, have been cut out from larger pictures, but their provenance is unknown and it is clear that at some stage they were adapted to fit the standard size of the set. The sixth later addition is a painting of George Clifford, third Earl of Cumberland (1558–1605), which has been painted on tropical hardwood, a material rarely used for portrait paintings in the 17th century.[9] Furthermore, the style of painting displays a smooth, blended quality that is characteristic of paintings of a later date than the rest of the set.

There is evidence to suggest that these six portraits were incorporated into the set in the 1790s, at the same time as the gilt spandrels and the carved wooden ribbons. We know from a surviving document that these decorative features were added in May 1793 when John Sackville, third Duke of Dorset (1745–99), paid the portrait painter and picture restorer Francis Parsons (d. 1804) for 'cleaning and Repairing forty old portraits on Pannels' and mending their frames.[10] Parsons' work also included adding 'new Gilt' and ribbons to each frame, 'label'd with the name and title of each portrait', and painting the 'Angle' of each with 'ornaments'. In addition, Parsons was paid for supplying 'one New Portrait' of the Earl of Cumberland, almost certainly the painting now in the group. All six of the additional paintings appear to have been added to the set by the end of the 1790s. When George Vertue (1684–1756) visited Knole in 1728 he made a list of the sitters in the set that does not include the names of the monarchs or Admiral Blake. However, the names of the last group are all listed along with the rest of the set in an inventory of the house dating from 1799.[11] Vertue's list did, however, include a portrait of Cumberland, which may indicate that the painting provided by Parsons was a replacement for an earlier version.[12]

The six later additions appear to have replica frames and it is probable that Parsons also supplied these at this time. The oak frames on the original 38 portraits, which are nailed to the front of the panels, appear to be contemporaneous with the paintings. In cases where the panels have curved away from the frames, bare wood can be seen at their edges, indicating that the frames were attached before the portraits were painted.[13] The frames on the six later additions are very similar, but the slightly different proportions of the egg-and-dart mouldings and the fact that they are generally in better condition than the others indicate that they are later copies. A layer structure beneath the gilding on the earlier frames similar to the gilding on the spandrels and the ribbons makes it likely

4

5

that Parsons also gilded or regilded the older frames.[14] He may also have been responsible for adapting the portraits of the monarchs and for producing the portrait labelled 'Admiral Blake'.

The Sources

All of the portraits from the original set are derived from pre-existing sources that are known to have been available by 1608, and many of the individuals depicted were standard figures in late Tudor and Jacobean portrait collections.[15] Twenty-three of the Knole sitters, for example, were represented in the famed portrait collection of John Lumley, first Baron Lumley (*c.* 1533–1609), when it was inventoried in 1590.[16] Given Dorset's social status, the makers of the set are likely to have had access to good-quality paintings of recent and contemporary figures, such as Lord Burghley, the Earl of Leicester, Salisbury and Sir Francis Walsingham. In the case of the latter two, who both appear in portraits after de Critz, Dorset's connections with that artist, by whom he himself was painted in around 1601, no doubt facilitated access to paintings or patterns. Good-quality painted prototypes seem to have been less readily available for the earlier sitters, however, and for the figures that were less frequently represented in English portrait collections. In the case of these portraits, inferior paintings appear to have been used, which accounts in part for the varying aesthetic quality of the pictures across the set. The portraits of Sir Thomas More and Thomas Cromwell, for example, are both ultimately derived from portraits by Hans Holbein the Younger, but their crude simplicity indicates that the immediate sources were paintings or perhaps prints at some remove from the originals (Fig. 5). The fact that pre-existing sources were

sought indicates that it was important for the portraits in the set to be recognisable. In some cases, the most authoritative sources were prints. The portrait of Wyclif, for example, corresponds to an anonymous woodcut included in Theodore Beza's *Les vrais pourtraits des hommes illustres* (1581; Fig. 6), and the one of Don John of Austria is based on an engraving in Emmanuel van Meteren's *Belgische ofte Nederlantsche historie, van onsen tijden* (1599). It is possible, however, that the Knole portraits were copied from other paintings derived from these graphic sources.

The Original Setting

When Vertue visited Knole in 1728, he observed 'a small gallery hung with Old pictures. on bord all alike in size & ornament'.[17] His list of the set comprises 37 names, the majority of which correspond with the extant paintings.[18] It is probable that he saw the set in what is now known as the Brown Gallery, which was at that time divided into two rooms: the First Gallery and the Horn Gallery.[19] The set probably made up the bulk of the 43 paintings recorded in the latter room in an inventory drawn up in 1730.[20] It was almost certainly in the Horn Gallery in 1786, in which year *The Tunbridge Wells Guide* listed a group of 'Illustrious Heads, in the Time of Henry VIII' among the paintings.[21] In 1799, portraits of all but two of the sitters in the current set were recorded in the Brown Gallery, by which time the partition had been removed.[22] The location of the set prior to the 18th century, however, is unrecorded. In *An Historical and Topographical Sketch of Knole*, first published in 1817, John Bridgman (steward at the house

6

7

8

from at least 1794) stated that the set had previously hung in the Cartoon Gallery.[23] The large copies of cartoons by Raphael that give this room its name were brought to Knole in around 1701 and, according to Bridgman, it was at this point that the portraits were removed.

The Cartoon Gallery is situated on the first floor at Knole, within the suite of state apartments created as part of the first earl's remodelling. Although the arrival of the cartoons significantly altered the appearance of the room, a substantial amount of the early 17th-century decoration survives, including the plasterwork ceiling, the painted cornice and architrave, and some ornamental carving.[24] The original polychrome scheme incorporated elements typical of Jacobean court fashion: classical pilasters and capitals, arabesques, painted allegorical figures and grotesques, and heraldic symbols, including carved Sackville leopards. The moulded plaster cornice that runs around the room has been decorated with a stencilled design of white and gold on a blue ground. On the north and east walls, the frieze has been obscured by a velvet wall covering, but the Jacobean scheme is still visible on the south and west walls (Fig. 7). In these areas, it is clear that the cornice brackets, placed around the room at intervals of approximately 73–84cm, served to define a series of rectangular spaces along the frieze, each measuring around 86.5cm in height. The brackets, which are visible above the textile wall covering, indicate that if the frieze originally continued in this way around the room, there would have been up to 52 of these spaces. Currently, 12 of the exposed spaces are occupied by paintings on canvas of flowers and fruit of a style popular in the Netherlands in the later 17th century. These paintings do not fit comfortably in the spaces and were clearly not made for this location. The existence of 11 more examples in the private Sackville collection makes it highly likely that they are the 'twenty-three Dutch paintings' that were brought to Knole along with other items from the palaces of Kensington and Whitehall in 1696 and were therefore installed in the frieze after this date.[25] The fact that the portraits are both contemporaneous with

the decoration in the frieze and of the correct size strongly indicates that it was the paintings in the Brown Gallery set that previously occupied these spaces.

In December 2015 a team of textile conservators led by Zenzie Tinker removed a small section of the velvet wall hanging from the east corner of the north wall, revealing a section of the frieze that had previously been obscured. Two empty spaces were discovered, each of a size large enough to fit a portrait from the set, along with its current moulded frame, confirming the continuation of the frieze around the room. In addition, the discovery of this section of the frieze has provided new information about the appearance of the original scheme. The newly discovered spaces are surrounded by painted black frames decorated with a gold strap-work design in a style typical of Jacobean decoration (Fig. 8). Furthermore, the shape of more of these frames can be made out beneath the velvet along at least part of the north wall and some of the top edges are partially visible above the hanging. In addition, the edge of the last frame before the fireplace can be seen in a break in the velvet. A similar frame remains intact around a heraldic panel in the frieze on the north side of the west bay window (Fig. 9). It is very likely that this element of the decorative frieze originally continued around the room. When installed in this location, therefore, the portraits would have been framed first by the egg-and-dart moulded frames and then by the black and gold frames, which were integral to the frieze. A gap of around 14cm between the newly discovered black frames would presumably have held a carved terminal figure, examples of which still flank the flower and fruit paintings on the opposite wall.

The Function

The argument presented above for the date of the set and its connection to Knole has relied heavily on physical evidence, but the likely function of the set and the choice of sitters also link it to the first Earl of Dorset. When he began work on Knole in 1605, Dorset was one

9

FIG 9 View of the Cartoon Gallery in which a heraldic frieze is visible on the north side of the west bay window, Knole, Kent
Photo: Ben Blossom, 2016

of England's leading courtiers. He had been Chancellor of the University of Oxford since 1591 and Lord Treasurer since 1599. He was keen to display the trappings of high office and to present himself as a man worthy of the high status that he had achieved.[26] His acquisition of Knole and subsequent remodelling were largely driven by his desire to present himself as an ideal courtier, partly through the creation of a fashionable and lavish decorative scheme.

The portrait set was one element in this self-fashioning. But the set also provided a retrospective view of the times through which Dorset had lived. The portraits of statesmen and bishops alluded to the fundamental changes brought about by the break with Rome. The paintings of foreign figures, such as Alexander Farnese, Duke of Parma, offered a reminder of some of the chief threats to the security of the nation. The set also celebrated national heroes, such as Sir Francis Drake, Sir John Norris and Charles Howard, first Earl of Nottingham, and commemorated other important contemporary figures too. The presence of Bacon and Wyclif can be explained by Dorset's position at the University of Oxford, which considered both alumni heroes. Inspired by the *Uomini Famosi* that Dorset had no doubt read about and even witnessed on the continent, the set seems to have had a moralising purpose. With the inclusion of 'fallen' men, such as the fourth Duke of Norfolk, enemies of the state, heroes and both Protestant and Catholic bishops, the set holds up a mirror to the nation's recent history, inviting lessons to be drawn. The inclusion of his own portrait in the set, derived from the painting by de Critz, commemorated Dorset's personal role in the national narrative. Through this portrait set, in which he himself was pictured among so many famous faces, Dorset sealed his posthumous legacy at the heart of his grand new residence.

Catherine Daunt has recently completed a DPhil at the University of Sussex on 'Portrait Sets in Tudor and Jacobean England' in collaboration with the National Portrait Gallery. She is Monument Trust Project Curator in the department of Prints and Drawings at the British Museum.

1. This research was undertaken by the author for her doctoral thesis, to which a catalogue of the paintings is appended. See Catherine Daunt, 'Portrait Sets in Tudor and Jacobean England', 2 vols., unpublished PhD thesis, University of Sussex, 2015.

2. In 2011 the paintings were given a date on the National Trust online catalogue of *c*. 1600. Alistair Laing discusses the date of the set in unpublished notes dating from 1998. See Alistair Laing, 'Knole: English, late 16th Century: the set of portraits of Famous Men in the Brown Gallery', Heinz Library and Archive, National Portrait Gallery.

3. Funded by the National Trust, the analysis was carried out by Ian Tyers over four days between July 2012 and January 2013. For the full results, see Ian Tyers, 'The Tree-Ring Analysis of 13 Panel Paintings from the Historical Portrait Set in the Brown Gallery, Sackville Collection, Knole', unpublished report, Report 566, Dendrochronology Consultancy Ltd., October 2012 and Ian Tyers, 'The Tree-Ring Analysis of 22 of the 44 Panel Paintings in the Historical Portrait Set in the Brown Gallery, Sackville Collection, Knole', unpublished report, Report 580, Dendrochronology Consultancy Ltd., March 2013.

4. Wood from this tree was identified in the panels used for the portraits of Don John of Austria and Sir Francis Drake. These panels were linked to a further four panels by wood from the other boards used in their construction (the panels in question show Henry Howard, Earl of Surrey; Sir Francis Walsingham; Charles III, Duke of Bourbon; and Henry I, Duke of Guise).

5. Only seven were still alive at this time: Richard Bancroft, Archbishop of Canterbury (d. 1610); Robert Cecil, Earl of Salisbury (d. 1612); Henry Howard, Earl of Northampton (d. 1614); Henry I, Duke of Montmorency (d. 1614); Thomas Egerton, Viscount Brackley (d. 1617); Charles Howard, Earl of Nottingham (d. 1624) and Thomas I Howard, Earl of Suffolk (d. 1626).

6. Tyers, 2013, op. cit., p. 52.

7. Charles J. Phillips, *History of the Sackville Family (Earls and Dukes of Dorset): Together with a description of Knole, early owners of Knole and a catalogue raisonné of the pictures and drawings at Knole*, 2 vols., London, 1929, vol. II, p. 423.

8. On the argument that it represents Fenner, see Richard Leathes, 'Farewell Admiral Blake: A long overdue welcome to Captain George Venour (Fenner)', unpublished research, 2011.

9. Tyers, 2012, op. cit., p. 1.

10. Jacob Simon, 'A Guide to Picture Frames at Knole, Kent', 1998, revised 2013 [accessed 13 March 2016: www.npg.org.uk/research/programmes/the-art-of-the-picture-frame/guides-knole].

11. George Vertue, 'Note Books II', *The Walpole Society*, vol. XX, 1931–32, pp. 50–51; Kent History and Library Centre (KHLC), U269/E4 and U269/E5.

12. Unlike the monarchs, Cumberland was not included in the 1799 inventory, but he was listed among the sitters in the set in H.N. Willis's *Biographical Sketches of Eminent Persons, whose portraits form part of the Duke of Dorset's collection at Knole*, London, 1795, pp. 68–72.

13. This can be seen clearly, for example, on the portrait of Charles Howard, Earl of Nottingham.

14. Daunt, op. cit., vol. I, p. 157.

15. Ibid, vol. I, pp. 150–53; vol. II, Table 8.

16. Ibid.

17. Vertue, op. cit., pp. 50–51.

18. For a comparison between Vertue's list and the current group, see Daunt, op. cit., vol. II, Table 9.

19. This was recently established by Emma Slocombe. See 'Ancient Furnishing: The Display and Alteration of Upholstered Seat Furniture and Textiles Associated with the Brown Gallery, Knole, in the Nineteenth Century', *Furniture History*, vol. L, 2014, pp. 297–325.

20. KHLC (number unknown), 'An Inventory of Goods at Knole Taken in Nov.r 1730'.

21. J. Sprange, *The Tunbridge Wells Guide; or An Account of the ancient and present State of that Place*, Tunbridge Wells, 1786, p. 187. In this guide, the Brown Gallery is listed as a separate room to the Horn Gallery, which indicates that the 'First Gallery' had been renamed by this point but that the partition had not yet been removed.

22. KHLC, U269/E5, ff. 15–16. The missing sitters are the Earl of Cumberland and the Earl of Salisbury, the portraits of whom may have been temporarily elsewhere, destroyed (in the case of Cumberland picture) or accidentally unrecorded.

23. John Bridgman, *An Historical and Topographical Sketch of Knole in Kent: With a Brief Genealogy of the Sackville Family*, London, 1817, p. 18.

24. See Dorian Church, 'The Cartoon Gallery, Knole', unpublished MA thesis, Courtauld Institute of Art, University of London, 1998.

25. KHLC, U269/O69/1, f. 2r. First suggested by Emma Slocombe.

26. Edward Town, 'A House "Re-Edified": Thomas Sackville and the Transformation of Knole, 1605–1608', unpublished PhD thesis, University of Sussex, 2010, pp. 17, 86.

1

A RICH INHERITANCE

LIONEL CRANFIELD'S LEGACY AT KNOLE

The connection between Knole and the textile merchant turned politician Lionel Cranfield has long been acknowledged, yet less attention has been paid to his role as patron. EDWARD TOWN and OLIVIA FRYMAN examine his contribution to the Stuart collections housed at Knole

IN 1637 RICHARD SACKVILLE, fifth Earl of Dorset (1622–77), married Frances Cranfield (*c.* 1623–87), the daughter of Lionel Cranfield, first Earl of Middlesex (1575–1645), a textile merchant turned courtier and politician who had made and lost a fortune during the reign of James I. This match produced seven sons and six daughters, the eldest of whom, Charles Sackville, succeeded his father as Earl of Dorset in 1677. Towards the end of her life, Lady Frances became the heir to her father's estate, including his Essex house, Copthall, where he had lived out his final years. The house, which was still furnished with many of the expensive possessions that Cranfield had bought at the height of his court career, thus passed into the Sackville family. In 1701, when Copthall was sold by the sixth earl, the choicest furnishings and artworks from the house were brought to Knole, where some of them remain today.

This connection between Lionel Cranfield (Fig. 1) and Knole has long been acknowledged, yet to date there has been no comprehensive study of his houses, furnishings, paintings and activities as a patron, or of how his possessions came to Knole. Previous studies have focused on either his political career or his architectural patronage.[1] This article presents new research on Cranfield's patronage, with an emphasis on his acquisition of rich furniture from London's leading craftsmen during the reign of James I. Using a series of inventories and the meticulous accounts of Cranfield's steward, Thomas Catchmay, it also charts the movement of some of his possessions from his property at Chelsea to Copthall and then to Knole. Knole lost much of its pre-Civil War collection in two forced sales ordered by Parliament in 1645 and 1646.[2] However, Cranfield's possessions came eventually to take their place, joining the Jacobean and Caroline furnishings that the sixth Earl of Dorset acquired as perquisites from the royal palaces.[3] This ensured that by the early 18th century Knole contained an extraordinary collection of high-status Stuart furniture, paintings and tapestries, some of which were subsequently introduced into the showrooms of the house.

FIG 1 *Lionel Cranfield, 1st Earl of Middlesex (1575–1645)*, 1620–24, Daniel Mytens the elder, (1590–1647) oil on canvas, 221 x 137.2cm, Knole, Kent Photo: © National Trust Images

Lionel Cranfield was the second son of the London mercer Thomas Cranfield (d. 1595). He was educated at St Paul's School and apprenticed to Richard Sheppard, a merchant who specialised in the sale of cloths, silks and taffetas. Described by his modern biographer, Menna Prestwich, as the 'rogue elephant' in the City, Cranfield 'had the ambition and the energy, the cleverness and the unscrupulousness to bring him to the top of the London business world'.[4] By the second decade of the 17th century, his success as a speculator had earned him a small fortune, and his abilities as a financier soon led to appointments at court. As Chief Surveyor of the Customs, Cranfield proved his worth by demonstrating to the crown how best to realise the value of customs leases. His appointments as Master of the Great Wardrobe (1618) and Master of the Court of Wards (1619) not only dramatically improved his income but also consolidated his position at court.[5] An advantageous second marriage to Anne Brett (d. 1670), a cousin of George Villiers, first Duke of Buckingham, in 1621 further enhanced his status. In the following year, shortly after becoming Lord Treasurer, he was created Earl of Middlesex. His position among the court elite seemed assured.

This rapid accumulation of titles and offices required Cranfield to act and live in a manner befitting his new-found status. The principal focus of his efforts was Chelsea House, which he acquired in 1619. Situated near what is now Beaufort Street and the King's Road, Chelsea House was one of the most significant riverside residences to the west of London, and had previously been owned by a succession of courtiers. It has been suggested that Sir Thomas More built a large house on this site in the 1520s. Certainly, the outline of an early Tudor building can be traced in drawings (now in the archives of Hatfield House) of the house made in around 1595 by the craftsman and surveyor John Symonds (d. 1597; Fig. 2).[6] These drawings also show that the east range contained a loggia on the ground floor and a gallery above, possibly added by Gregory Fiennes, tenth Baron Dacre (1539–94), who lived in the house up until his death. His wife bequeathed the house to Robert Cecil,

first Earl of Salisbury (1563–1612), who toyed with the idea of enlarging it: there are two alternative proposals for this, produced by William Spicer in around 1595, in the archives of Hatfield (Fig. 3).[7] In the event, Cecil decided in 1599 to sell the house to Henry Clinton, second Earl of Lincoln (1539–1616), who in turn sold it to Sir Arthur Gorges (1557–1625). It was from Gorges that Cranfield bought the property in 1619.[8] Although this rapid succession in ownership makes the precise sequence of development difficult to follow, it is clear that by 1623 – the date of John Thorpe's plan of Chelsea at Sir John Soane's Museum (Fig. 4) – Chelsea House had undergone a substantial transformation under Cranfield's guidance. It is thanks to the survival of a number of Cranfield's account books and papers from this period that is it possible to attribute this work, at least in part, to the court architect Inigo Jones (1573–1652).[9]

Cranfield had known Jones since his time as a City speculator, when the two were members of the Mitre Tavern circle. In 1611 both had provided verses in celebration of Thomas Coryate's famous travel journal, *Coryats Crudities*.[10] Jones's earliest involvement at Chelsea House can be dated to April 1620, when he wrote to Cranfield recommending the stonemason John Medhurst.[11] This letter may relate to the construction of the well-known Doric gateway, dated to 1621, that was erected in the garden at Chelsea House and was later transported to Lord Burlington's house at Chiswick.[12] The elaborate drawing for the gate, now in the RIBA collection, is inscribed by Jones as 'for the M: of the Wardes at Chelsey 1621' (Fig. 6). Previously, it has been assumed that the gateway was a discrete embellishment to the house, but it is now clear that it formed part of a much larger project undertaken by Jones for Cranfield. The accounts in the Cranfield papers relating to the building work at Chelsea survive for 1623, when work was nearing completion and activity was focused on the ground floor of the garden side of the house. Entries in Catchmay's account book record payments to the plasterer Richard Talbot 'for work by him done in the lower roomes by direction of Mr Inigo Jones'. Payments to the mason Richard Lowellin were to be made by Jones, 'by whose direction this money is paid', while the works undertaken by the master carpenter Ralph Brice were to be completed 'according to c[er]rtaine articles of agreement made betwixt him and Mr S[u]rveior'.[13]

In the bird's-eye view of Chelsea House produced by Kip and Knyff in around 1707, the building is not instantly recognisable as a Jones design (Fig. 5). Nevertheless, it is clear from Thorpe's ground plan of 1623 that Jones's chief task at Chelsea was to regularise the south facade through the addition of a centrally placed porch and symmetrically positioned bays with uniform fenestration.[14] The gallery range on the east side recorded by Symonds was removed, so that the range was symmetrical with the adjacent service wing.[15] To carry out this work, Cranfield employed leading craftsmen, many of whom also worked for the Office of the King's Works. For example, when he came to procure building materials for the chapel, he turned to Nicholas Stone, who, like Jones, was a frequent guest at Cranfield's table at Chelsea (Cran-

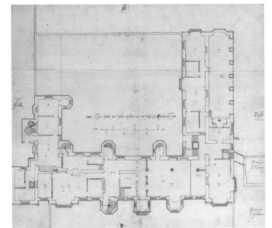

2

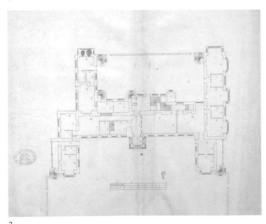

3

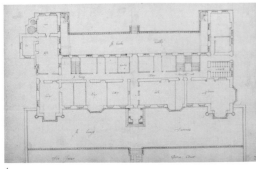

4

field later employed him on building projects at Copthall).[16] Francis Carter – a figure described by Howard Colvin as one of the few subordinates of Jones in the Office of Works with abilities as an architectural designer – acted alongside Jones in a supervisory role at Chelsea.[17]

The interior at Chelsea was completed to the highest standard. Decorative painting was undertaken by Richard Isaacson (1594–1659) and Rowland Bucket (1571–1638/39), both of whom were prominent members of the Painter-Stainers' Company of London.[18] Cranfield's furnishings at Chelsea were recorded in an inventory of the house taken in 1622, a remarkably detailed document that lists not only the contents of every room but also the names of the family members and servants who inhabited them.[19] It is likely that the inventory was compiled by Richard Colbeck, Cranfield's yeoman of the wardrobe at Chelsea. Colbeck, who was a trained upholsterer, was also a senior figure at the Great Wardrobe and effectively ran things there on Cranfield's behalf.[20] The inventory reveals that Chelsea House had a suite of staterooms, a great chamber, an adjoining bedchamber, a drawing room and a dining room, all of them richly furnished in accordance with their public and ceremonial functions. The great chamber was equipped with a great table, two great chairs, eight back chairs, 12 high stools and two low stools (both sets upholstered in crimson figured satin), a court cupboard that would have been used for a display of plate, and tapestries of the story of Noah. The withdrawing chamber was equally richly furnished with tapestries of the story of Diana and a suite of chairs and stools, all upholstered in carnation velvet, laced with carnation silk and silver – as was the furniture in the bedchamber adjoining, creating a continuous suite that showcased Cranfield's wealth and sophistication.[21]

In 1621 Cranfield ordered an exceptionally opulent suite of furniture for the lying-in of his wife ahead of the birth of their first son, James, in December of that year. This important occasion was given even greater significance when it was decided that James I would come to Chelsea to christen his newborn namesake and godson.[22] Cranfield therefore chose the best craftsmen, among them Oliver Browne and John Baker, who, as upholsterers to the Great Wardrobe, were responsible for supplying furnishings to the king himself.[23] Their bill shows that the lying-in suite included 'a verie large Sparver' or canopy, 'beinge made both teaster, head cloth, double vallances & curtens of damaske laced with a rich lace of gold and silver', an accompanying pallet canopy of 'Crimson satten ymbrodred sutable to the other great sparver the curtene being of Crimson & white damaske laced upon both sides wth lace of gold & silver', presumably for a lady in waiting to attend upon Lady Cranfield, and a cradle of crimson velvet and satin embroidered with gold, also with a canopy of crimson damask embroidered to match the sparver. There was also a set of matching seat furniture,

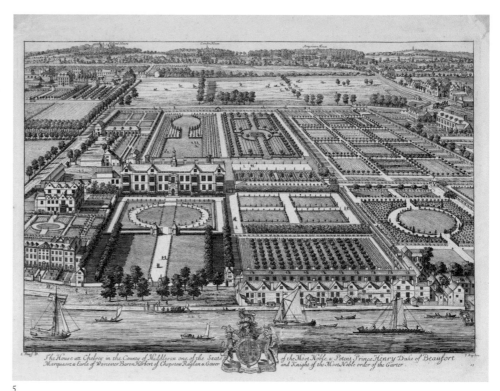

5

consisting of two great chairs, eight high stools, two low stools, one foot stool, one long cushion and one square cushion.[24] The magnificent effect of this profusion of finely upholstered furniture was not lost on observers. John Chamberlain, writing to Dudley Carleton, noted that Lady Cranfield, 'is saide to lie in very gorgeously, and (yf all be true) far beyond the qualitie they were in not longe since'.[25] Cranfield's metamorphosis from City merchant to great courtier was complete.

In acquiring this expensive furniture for Chelsea House, Cranfield made good use of his experience as a textile merchant and of his position as Master of the Great Wardrobe to buy goods for the best price. His purchase of two sets of tapestries in early 1620 is a case in point. In October 1619 one six-piece set depicting the story of Diana was recorded as being in Colbeck's custody within the Great Wardrobe.[26] Five months later it had been sold to Cranfield for the very reasonable sum of £257 12s.[27] At the same time, he also purchased a seven-piece set of the story of Noah from the Great Wardrobe at a cost of £260 8s.[28] It is evident that these were Cranfield's most prestigious tapestries and that they were purchased specifically for the furnishing of the withdrawing room and the great chamber at Chelsea.[29] Cranfield was also careful to ensure that he was not being overcharged for even the smallest item. When he received Browne and Baker's bill for the lying-in suite, he ensured that it

6

7

was checked by Colbeck before he made payment. While the original bill came to £52 7s 6d, Colbeck amended it to £48 5s 6d.[30] In addition, Cranfield bought goods directly from other merchants who specialised in fitting out the houses of wealthy courtiers.[31] At Chelsea he used Hugh Goddard (*c.* 1569–*c.* 1624), a London draper who supplied extravagantly upholstered furnishings to leading courtiers. A schedule of Goddard's bills, dating from between September 1620 and November 1622, that survives among Cranfield's official Wardrobe papers shows that he was responsible for providing the majority of the upholstered suites at Chelsea, as well as more quotidian items, such as rush matting, 'Bristol' carpets, course rugs and blankets.[32] However, Goddard's bills were for upholstering the furniture only, indicating that the extremely expensive textiles were probably sourced by Cranfield and Colbeck through the Great Wardrobe.[33]

In addition to his work managing the furnishings at Chelsea, Colbeck was also responsible for Cranfield's picture collection at the house. He was sent by Cranfield to Charlton House to purchase 38 pictures from Sir

Adam Newton (d. 1630). These pictures were bought for £95 10s and included 'a great peece of the deluge' (£15), a small painting of 'Pillatts washing his hands' (£7), 'a large night peece on Cloth' (£10), 'a larg peece on borde of the prodigall' (£8) and a 'peece on borde of St Anthonyes temtatione'.[34] This opportunistic purchase of pictures en bloc seems to have been in keeping with Cranfield's collecting practices, which never extended to the acquisition of Old Master paintings or antiquities. Perhaps the most interesting of the paintings at Chelsea were the pictures that hung in the hall of the London and Antwerp custom houses, a forthright allusion to Cranfield's mercantile past.[35] His family and court connections were also well represented. The gallery at Chelsea House was hung with full-length portraits of James I, Prince Charles, Lady Cranfield and Lady Carey (Cranfield's daughter Martha, Countess of Monmouth).[36] There were also half-length portraits of Cranfield's mother, of Mrs Osborne (Cranfield's sister-in-law by his first marriage), of Richard Martin (a lawyer who was a close friend of Cranfield and a member of the Mitre circle) and of 'Lady Fearne', along with a picture of Cleopatra and a small picture of the Passion.[37]

By 1624, Cranfield's improvements at Chelsea had given the house a value of £8,000 – £5,000 more than he had paid for it in 1619.[38] However, his enjoyment of life there was short lived. During the Parliament of 1624, Cranfield was impeached on charges of corruption, stripped of his offices in government and burdened with fines so heavy that he would never recover his position. In 1625 he was forced to sell Chelsea House and live out his days in frustrated exile at Copthall. Cranfield's furnishings, paintings and household goods were packed up under the careful supervision of Catchmay. Ever mindful of their worth, especially in his new circumstances, Cranfield wrote to Catchmay asking him to 'take spetial care there bee not so much as a truncke taken out of the howse but yow see it opened & send me the inventory allonge with it', adding that his prized hangings 'in the best with-

8a

8b

8c

drawing chamb[e]r of Dyana be browght if there be Convenient Carraig[e]'.³⁹ The finest pieces from Chelsea were installed in the staterooms at Copthall. The Noah and Diana tapestries appear in the list of goods transported there in 1625 and in two inventories of 1674 and 1679, in which they are recorded as hanging in the great chamber and the withdrawing chamber.⁴⁰ Similarly, the rich carnation velvet furniture from the withdrawing room and bedchamber at Chelsea appears in a Copthall inventory of around 1628, where it is listed as being in the 'withdrawing room, next the Chamber of State'.⁴¹

In 1701 Copthall was sold by Cranfield's grandson the sixth Earl of Dorset and much of the house's contents were transported to the Sackville family seat at Knole. Although 80 years old by this time, Cranfield's furniture would undoubtedly have appealed to Dorset, who, as mentioned above, acquired numerous historical pieces of furniture from the royal palaces through his right to claim old or unwanted goods as perquisites. During the course of the 18th century, Cranfield's furnishings and paintings were subsumed into the collection at Knole, the finest pieces being chosen for display in the show rooms of the house. Since then, their distinct history has largely been forgotten, some pieces have been lost and others altered beyond recognition.

Nevertheless, there are several surviving pieces that can plausibly be identified with Cranfield through close examination of inventories and lists detailing the transportation of goods. Of Cranfield's pictures, for example, the painting 'of a usurer' recorded in the Great Gallery at Copthall in 1625 is probably the painting that hangs in the lobby of the Brown Gallery, today titled *The Miser* (Fig. 7). The 'foulding picture' of Martin Luther 'and others' that hung in the closet room that overlooked the chapel at Copthall would appear to correspond to the three pictures formerly in triptych format in the Brown Gallery of Philip Melanchthon, of Martin Luther and

9

Johann Bugenhagen Pommer, and of Rodolphus Agricola and Desiderius Erasmus (Figs. 8a, 8b & 8c). The 'picture of Christ on the Sea', also from Copthall, might be identified as the picture of *The Calling of St Peter and St Andrew* in the chapel at Knole (Fig. 9). The portraits of James I, Prince Charles and Lady Carey that hung in the gallery at Chelsea may be those now displayed in the Leicester Gallery. Some of Cranfield's tapestries from Chelsea can also be identified. The set of six tapestries of the story of Noah that he purchased in 1620 are probably those recorded in the King's Bedchamber at Knole in an inventory of 1706 and may be related to one surviving tapestry depicting the same subject after designs by Michiel Coxcie that are now in the private apartments (Fig. 10).⁴² It is also likely that Cranfield's Diana tapestries are those by François Spiering (*c.* 1550–1630), after designs by Karl van Mander (1548–1606), that now hang at Knole in the Venetian Ambassador's Bedroom and depict the stories of Diana and Actaeon and Niobe's Pride.

Furthermore, the inventories suggest that Knole's renowned Spangled Bed and its matching chairs and stools were also owned by Cranfield and can be identified as part of Lady Anne's rich lying-in suite (Fig. 11).⁴³ The suite was moved in 1625 from Chelsea to Copthall, where it was installed in the chamber of state.⁴⁴ An inventory of the house taken in *c.* 1628 lists:

> 1 Rich Sparver of Crimson Satten Embrodered wth Cloth of Silver & Lyned wth Crymson & White damaske & laced wth silver & gold lace
> 1 greate Square Canopie wth damaske Curtaines double laced
> 1 Round Cannopie wth damake Curtaines Sutable
> 12 fethers
> 1 head Cloth to the Square Canopie
> 1 Chaire of State
> 1 great Chaire
> 8 high stooles} all of Crimson Satten embrodred wth Cloth of Silver wth Silke and gold fringe

FIG 9 *The Calling of St Peter and St Andrew, c.* 1600, artist unknown, oil on panel, 75 x 100.5cm, Knole, Kent Photo: Ben Blossom, 2016

FIG 10 Detail from a tapestry depicting the story of Noah after designs by Michiel Coxcie (1499–1592), Knole, Kent Photo: Ben Blossom, 2016

11

2 low stooles
1 foote stole
1 longe Cushion
1 Backe Chaire} of Crimson Satten embrodred w[th
cloth of Silver
1 Square Cushion
…
1 Crimson Taffeta quille [quilt?]
1 fether Bed & boulster
1 paire of downe pillowes
1 Matteris
1 pallett bedsted[45]

By the 1670s, the majority of the suite was still at the house, in the 'King's chamber' (also known as 'ye Rich Chamber'). Two inventories, dated 1674 and 1679, record a 'great Sparver Beed dubell vallens five great Cuirtaines testor & head Cloth of Crimson Sattin Imbroidered with Cloth of tissue with gould & ewes lynd with read & whit damaske with a depe gould and silver fringe'.[46] There was also a 'read & white dammaske beed' decorated with gold and silver lace and a deep gold and silver fringe with a counterpoint of red satin embroidered with cloth of tissue. Also listed were two great chairs, one back chair, eight high stools, two low stools and one footstool, all upholstered in crimson satin embroidered with cloth of tissue and edged with gold and silver fringe.[47] The fuller description of the textiles given in these inventories enables a link to be made with the Spangled Bed

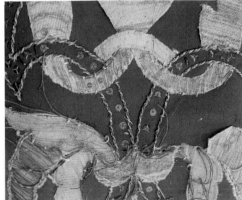

12

and the accompanying furniture at Knole. In particular, the 'ewes' or 'owes' (presumably a a misspelling of 'eyes' or 'o's' [i.e. a round shape]) set on the embroidery of the sparver bed are almost certainly the spangles (made from tiny silver and silver gilt sequins) that give the bed its name (Fig. 12).[48] When new, these spangles, together with the gold and silver embroidery, would have glittered spectacularly, especially when seen by candlelight. The inventories also refer to embroiderd cloth of silver or tissue, which can almost certainly be identified as the appliqué strapwork on the Spangled Bed. Although this appears to be buff silk, recent conservation has shown that the strapwork is in fact very degraded cloth of silver. The 1679 inventory also makes reference to embroidery of 'gold twist' on the sparver. This corresponds to the thick twisted gold thread couched onto the appliqué decoration seen on the bed today. By 1706, the bed appears to have obtained its current name when it was listed as 'One Crimson Sattin Spangl'd Bed with Gold and Crimson Fringe' in store with other items from Copthall in the Wardrobe at Knole.[49]

At present, the Spangled Bed is undergoing conservation as part of the Inspired by Knole project. Over the last two years a number of important discoveries have been made. Current investigations have confirmed earlier suspicions that the bed is not all of one piece and was possibly put together in its current configuration by the sixth Earl of Dorset after he inherited Copthall, or when the bed was put up at Knole at some point between 1730 and 1765.[50] The tester and headboard are almost certainly not original to the suite and the bed curtains have been cut and pieced, suggesting some significant alterations over the last 300 years. Although conservation is still underway, it now seems likely that the Spangled Bed is an amalgam of Lady Cranfield's great sparver, square canopy and round canopy from her lying-in suite.[51] The suite was one of Cranfield's most prestigious and costly commissions from Browne and Baker. Its partial survival over almost four centuries and at three different houses is testimony to the importance ascribed to it by successive generations.

Up until his death in 1645 Cranfield persistently petitioned the crown for a return to office, but was continually disappointed. He spent his remaining days in melancholic fashion, stalking his house at Copthall, convinced that his servants were swindling his depleted assets away. His meteoric rise to wealth, power and privilege ended in disgrace and disillusionment. Yet Cranfield's patronage and his brief but magnificent life at Chelsea live on in the collections at Knole. Together with the sixth Earl of Dorset's own acquisitions, Cranfield's furnishings and pictures are some of the most important and rare survivals from the world of the early Stuart court. As the research and conservation work for the Inspired by Knole project continues, it is hoped that further new discoveries will make it possible to identify more pieces that belonged to Lionel Cranfield and to understand more fully his contribution to the unrivalled Stuart collections at Knole.

Edward Town is a Postdoctoral Research Associate at the Yale Center for British Art. Olivia Fryman is Exhibition Assistant Curator at the Royal Collection Trust.

1. Previous published studies of Cranfield have been largely biographical and have concentrated on his career as a courtier and mercer. See for example, Menna Prestwich, *Cranfield: Politics and Profits Under the Early Stuarts*, Oxford, 1966. For a study of his houses, see Rebecca Roberts, '"Two meane fellows grand projectors": The self-projection of Sir Arthur Ingram and Lionel Cranfield, Earl of Middlesex, 1600–1645, with a particular reference to their houses', unpublished PhD thesis, Teeside University, 2012. A short piece on Cranfield's furniture at Chelsea was published by the authors in *Furniture History Society Newsletter*, May 2011.
2. Kent History and Library Centre (hereafter KHLC), U269 O10/1; U269 O10/2. The young Charles Sackville (later sixth Earl of Dorset but then styled as Lord Buckhurst) was present at the sale and was able to buy back some items, but this did little to stem the tide of objects leaving the house. His purchases included nine pictures of the Story of Malta from the Great Hall (£3); the entire contents of the 'Greate Dyning Roome' (i.e. the Great Chamber or Ballroom) (£13 1s 4d); 18 pictures in the 'Passage where the Emperors head hangs' (£1 16s); the entire 18 of the 'withdrawing chamber to the Rich Gallery' (the Reynolds Room) (£8); a gilt bed with the Earl of Dorset's arms in an inner chamber to the 'Damaske Bed chamber' (later known as the Spangled Bed Chamber) (10s); two trunks (£1 10s); a child's chair of crimson velvet (10s) from the Standing Wardrobe; two turkey carpets; and a handful of other small furnishings from elsewhere in the house.
3. On Dorset's royal perquisites see Olivia Fryman, 'Rich Pickings: The Royal Bed as a Perquisite, 1660–1760', *Furniture History*, vol. L, 2014, pp. 119–36; Christopher Rowell, 'The King's Bed and its Furniture at Knole', *Apollo*, November 2004, pp. 58–65; Gervase Jackson-Stops, 'A Courtier's Collection: The sixth Earl of Dorset's Furniture at Knole', *Country Life*, 2 June 1977, pp. 1496–97; Gervase Jackson-Stops, 'Purchase and Perquisites: The sixth Earl of Dorset's Furniture at Knole', *Country Life*, 9 June 1977, pp. 1621–22; Ralph Edwards, 'A Set of Royal Furniture Restored at Knole', *Connoisseur*, June 1968, pp. 69–71.
4. Prestwich, op. cit., p. 55.
5. Prestwich states that Cranfield's income was £6,000. It rose to twice this amount when he became Master of the Wardrobe. See Prestwich, op. cit., p. 260.

6. Hatfield House Archive, CMP II 9; CMP II 10. For Symonds, see J. Summerson, 'Three Elizabethan Architects', *Bulletin of the John Rylands Library*, vol. XL, 1957, pp. 209–25.
7. Walter H. Godfrey, *Survey of London, Vol. IV, The Parish of Chelsea (Part 2)*, London, 1913, p. 22; Hatfield House Archive, CPM II 15; CPM II 16.
8. An inventory of 1606 records the contents of the house belonging to Henry Clinton, second Earl of Lincoln. See The National Archives (hereafter TNA), SP 14/23, f. 21 et seq. The Calendar of State Papers suggests that the contents of this inventory belonged to Lord Norris, but this is an error. Francis Norris, later first Earl of Berkshire (1579–1622), was Clinton's stepson and was in residence at Chelsea at this point.
9. For Cranfield's changes to the property, see Roberts, op. cit., pp. 152–62, and John Harris & Gordon Higgot, *Inigo Jones: Complete Architectural Drawings*, London, 1989, pp. 128–31.
10. *The Odcombian Banquet: Dished foorth by Thomas the Coriat, and Served in by a number of Noble Wits in prayse of his Crudities and Crambe too*, London, 1611.
11. The letter was first published in Randall Davies, *The Greatest House at Chelsey*, London, 1914, p. 143; KHLC, U269/1 E2.
12. Harris & Higgot, op. cit., pp. 128–31.
13. KHLC, U269/1 AP43.
14. John Summerson, 'The Book of Architecture of John Thorpe in Sir John Soane's Museum', *Walpole Society*, vol. XL, 1966, pp. 63–64.
15. The plans are reproduced in Godfrey, op. cit., pp. 20–21.
16. Payments were made both to Stone and his son, William, for 'provision of white and black marble for the paving of the Chappell'. See KHLC, U269/1 AP45. For a list of guests at Chelsea in spring 1623, see KHLC, U269/1 AP51.
17. Howard Colvin, *A Biographical Dictionary of British Architects, 1600–1840*, New Haven & London, 1995, p. 228. For example, craftsmen such as the joiner Robert Suead worked according to 'Mr Carters direction'. See KHLC, U269/1 AP43. This may have been the same 'Suede' who submitted a bill for joiners work for the Earl of Holland for his repairs to Holland House Kensington, *c.* 1635, for 'waenscording the loier grett rome'. See TNA, E192/15/20.
18. Edward Town, 'A Biographical Dictionary of London Painters: 1547–1625', *Walpole Society*, vol.

LXXVI, 2014, pp. 46, 117.
19. Lambeth Palace Library (hereafter LPL), MS 1228.
20. Prestwich, op. cit., p. 231. At Chelsea, it is clear that Colbeck's responsibilities went beyond managing the existing furnishings, for the accounts record that during the renovations at the house Colbeck was instructed to direct work in Jones's absence. See KHLC, U269/1 AP43.
21. LPL, MS 1228, f. 51.
22. Norman McClure (ed.), *The Letters of John Chamberlain*, vol. II, Philadelphia, 1939, p. 417.
23. On Browne and Baker, see Geoffrey Beard, *Upholsterers & Interior Furnishing in England 1530–1840*, London & New Haven, 1997, p. 47.
24. KHLC, U269/1 OW 46. By 1622 the lying-in suite was in store in the Wardrobe at Chelsea. See LPL, MS 1228, f. 56. 'Sparver' is an old fashioned term derived from the French word *espervier* sometimes used in the 17th century to describe a suspended canopy over a bed. Sparvers were traditionally made by tapering strips of fabric formed in a bell shape and fitted to a disc, but by the 17th century they could be square, rectangular or conical in shape. They were usually combined with a head cloth, curtains and valences and topped with feather plumes. See Clive Edwards, *Encyclopaedia of Furnishing Textiles, Floorcoverings and Home Furnishing Practices, 1200–1950*, London, 2007, p. 197.
25. McClure (ed.), op. cit., p. 436.
26. KHLC, U269/1 OW 57.
27. KHLC, U269/1 OW 46. We are grateful to Helen Wyld for sharing her expertise and knowledge as to the relative costs of tapestries during the period.
28. KHLC, U269/1 OW 46.
29. LPL, MS 1228, f. 57.
30. KHLC, U246/1 OW 46
31. Joseph Foster (ed.), *London Marriage Licenses, 1521–1869*, London, 1887, p. 556; A. H. Johnson, *The History of the Worshipful Company of the Drapers of London*, 5 vols., Oxford, 1914–1922, vol. 4. 1922, p. 458; Percival Boyd, *Roll of the Drapers' Company of London*, London, 1934, p. 76. For a list of the goods supplied in 1610 by Goddard to Gray Brydges, fifth Baron Chandos (1580–1621), comprising a bed of crimson embroidered with gold, two chairs and four stools, which came to £232 12s 9d, see London Metropolitan Archives, CLA/024/02/044.
32. KHLC, U269/1 OW35.
33. For example, Cranfield purchased textiles from the mercer Samuell Gouldsmith. See KHLC, U269/1 OW49.
34. KHLC, U269/1 F8 ('A notte of the picktures brought from Charlton').
35. LPL, MS 1228, f. 58.
36. The portraits of James I, Prince Charles and Lady Carey are possibly pictures NT 129891, NT 129879 and NT 129889 in the Leicester Gallery, Knole.

37. LPL, MS 1228/52.
38. Prestwich, op. cit., p. 600.
39. KHLC, U269/1 E187.
40. LPL, MS 1228; KHLC, U269/1 E16 (Inventory of Copthall, *c.* 1628); KHLC, U269 E198/2 ('Inventory of all ye goods in Copthall within ye house', 24 October 1679); KHLC, U269 E79/2 (list of goods moved from Copthall to Knole).
41. KHLC, U269/1 E16, f. 3.
42. KHLC, U269 E79/2. The dimensions are sufficiently specific to allow the identification of individual tapestries. The second tapestry (409 x 386cm) is *The Drunkenness of Noah*; the third (409 x 409cm) is the *Embarkation of the Arc*; the seventh (409 x 549cm) is *Noah Building the Arc*. The 1706 inventory also records 'One peice of Noahs Ark Tapistry belongs to the Suite in the Kings Chamber 13. Foot deep' in the Wardrobe at Knole. The authors are grateful to Helen Wyld for her assistance in identifying these tapestries. Cranfield's set of tapestries depicting the story of Noah seems to have been combined with another set at the house showing the same subject.
43. The authors are grateful to Emma Slocombe, who first made the connection between the Spangled Bed and the beds listed in the 1674 and 1679 inventories of Copthall. Her expertise on the textiles of the Spangled Bed and furniture at Knole and the documents relating to the house has been invaluable throughout the research and writing of this article.
44. KHLC, U269/1 E16 (Inventory of Copthall, *c.* 1628).
45. KHLC, U269/1 E16, fols. 2–3
46. KHLC, U269 E198/2, 1674; U269 E198/2, 1679.
47. KHLC, U269 E198/2, ff. 20–21; U269, E198/2, f. 4.
48. The spangles are described as 'ewes' or 'owes' in the 1674 inventory and as 'oys' in the 1679 inventory, suggesting that both are a misspelling of eyes or o's. Throughout both inventories the spelling is extremely eccentric and inconsistent.
49. KHLC, U269 E79/2. This inventory is at Knole and known only through a transcription (file number 170.002). This is a fair copy of KHLC, U269 E3.
50. For discussions about the dating and composition of the bed, see Beard, op. cit., p. 90 and Peter Thornton, 'The Royal State Bed', *Connoisseur*, June 1977, pp. 137–47.
51. For recent discoveries during the conservation of the bed, see 'Analytical Report: Hangings of a spangled bed, Knole, Sevenoaks, Kent', 3 December 2015 and National Trust, Knole Conservation Bulletins, November 2014, February 2016 and March 2016.

1

FROM PARIS TO KNOLE

THE THIRD DUKE OF DORSET AND THE FIRST EARL WHITWORTH AS DIPLOMATIC PATRONS AND COLLECTORS

Knole is famous for its 17th-century upholstered furniture drawn from English royal palaces. But, as CHRISTOPHER ROWELL and WOLF BURCHARD reveal, it also houses several examples of later Parisian furniture, acquired by two British ambassadors to France

JUST AS CHARLES SACKVILLE, sixth Earl of Dorset (1638–1706) brought back important furniture from France – including the famous table and flanking stands, attributed to Pierre Gole, which were supposedly presents from Louis XIV – so his great-grandson, John Frederick Sackville, third Duke of Dorset (1745–99), and Charles Whitworth, first (and last) Baron, Viscount and Earl Whitworth (1752–1825), also acquired works of art during their respective embassies to the court of Louis XVI and the First French Republic.[1] This article focuses on these two sophisticated patrons and collectors, who were united by friendship, by diplomacy, by marriage to the same woman (Whitworth married the duke's widow, Arabella Cope) and by Knole.[2] It illuminates objects which have tended to be eclipsed by the significant 17th-century furnishings of the house, much of it royal, for which Knole is justly famous.[3]

The third Duke of Dorset was interested in the arts of France long before he went to Paris as ambassador. He was presumably 'Monsieur Le Comte Dorset', who on 28 July 1768, was charged the huge sum of 5,339 livres by the Parisian menuisier, Louis Delanois (1731–92), who supplied rich chairs, sofas and beds.[4] He also bought Sèvres porcelain in 1770, acquiring from the *marchand-mercier*, Jean Dulac, a dessert service in the pattern '*rubans bleu céleste*', which was reacquired by the National Trust for Knole in 2005.[5] Indeed, Dorset was a regular customer of the Sèvres manufactory.[6] His uncle, the second duke, as Earl of Middlesex, had been a founder member of the Society of Dilettanti, to which the third duke was elected in 1776. His prime qualification was extensive travel in Italy in 1770.[7] A document begun in 1771 and augmented in 1774 and 1778 is headed initially: 'An Account of the Number and Value of the Pictures, Busts, &c. Purchased by His Grace John Frederick Sackville, Duke of Dorset, in Rome in the year 1770'.[8] This reveals that he formed his collections of pictures, watercolours, pastels and antique sculpture under the tutelage of the dealers and *ciceroni* Thomas Jenkins and James Byres, and that he was capable of paying the huge sums of money that they demanded, including '35. A Capital Picture of Lucrecia by Guido Reni' for the then colossal figure of £750. His acquisitions included those 'Bought of Vitturi, A Venitian [sic] Nobleman, at Venice in April 1771' and amounted *in toto* to £5,502 15s. The list continues under the heading 'Pictures bought by His Grace in London' in 1774–75 and 1778. The later entries encompass his extensive patronage of Gainsborough and Reynolds, including 'His Graces own Picture, Whole Length' at £157.10.0 by the latter.[9] Its carved and gilded frame with gadrooned top edges was supplied by Thomas Vials of Leicester Square in 1769 at a cost of 25 guineas.[10]

Dorset took an English mistress with him on the Grand Tour, the notorious courtesan Anne 'Nancy' Parsons, Mrs Horton, later Viscountess Maynard, although his love of art, dancing, opera and music is indelibly associated with Giovanna Zanerini (*c.* 1753–1801), known as La Baccelli and to the duke as Jannette.[11] She lived at Knole in a tower of her own – still endearingly called Shelley's [a corruption of Baccelli's] Tower[12] – and was famous for her good looks, her charm, her kindness and her undoubted ability on the musical stage at a time when ballet and opera were interlinked. Her informal head-and-shoulders portrait as a Bacchante, for which Reynolds was paid £26 5s, is still at Knole (Sackville Collection), but the magnificent Gainsborough full-length of her dancing in costume, which cost £60, is now at Tate Britain (see p. 55, John Chu, Fig. 4). At Paris, La Baccelli is said to have worn the duke's diamond-incrusted Garter (awarded in 1788) as a headband during her performances at the Opera. Her sculptural 'Bust', listed among the duke's purchases for £21 in 1778, and exhibited at the Royal Academy in 1781, has disappeared, but her life-size nude plaster statue (*c.* 1781; Fig. 2) is attributed to the same Veronese sculptor, Giovanni Battista Locatelli (a pupil of G.A. Finali), who assisted Nollekens and taught J.C.F. Rossi in London between 1778 and 1790.[13]

FIG 1 Mantel clock with figure of Omphale, *c.* 1800, Paris, gilt bronze, 51.2 x 44.5 x 11.cm, Knole, Kent (Sackville Collection)
Photo: Ben Blossom, 2016

2

France. He was 'generally liked for his sympathetic nature' and was, according to his steward, 'at all times the kindest in the world'.[19] On the flip side, he was the butt of much satire and said to be 'not in possession of any brains'.[20] His biographer concludes that he 'was an indolent and unremarkable ambassador to France',[21] while Horace Walpole called him 'a proverb of insufficience', declaring: 'The French could not desire a man more qualified to be a dupe.'[22]

As he progressed from his embassy at the hôtel de Charost in Paris to Versailles and then from one of the palace's antechambers to the next, Dorset spent no less than 17 Louis d'or in tipping Swiss guards, valets and servants until he finally reached the State Bedchamber for an introductory audience with Louis XVI. This substantial sum is carefully recorded in the spidery handwriting of the Sieur Desequeville, Secrétaire ordinaire du Roi, in charge of diplomatic audiences.[23] Dorset became a particular friend of Marie-Antoinette, whom he called 'Mrs. B[ourbon].' in his correspondence. Their friendship is hardly surprising given his reputation as a man irresistible to women. From Paris he wrote a series of letters, valuable now in the light of the impending Revolution, to his former mistress, Georgiana, wife of the fifth duke of Devonshire,[24] while his reports to the Foreign Office are full of the gossip of the court, exhibiting little sense of the impending extinction of the French monarchy.[25] While in Paris he continued to patronise the Sèvres factory, which delivered a dinner service to '*M. l'Ambassadeur d'Angleterre*' on 17 December 1784.[26]

Locatelli also carved an 'intensely erotic' marble *Reclining Venus* (Duke of Wellington Collection, Stratfield Saye), the probable plaster model of which, 'Venus on a Couch', was exhibited in 1779.[14] The alluring depiction of La Baccelli at Knole was described by early National Trust room guides as 'an old friend of the family'.[15] It depicts her reclining naked, turning her elegantly coiffed head towards the viewer. The composition is based on the Roman marble Hermaphrodite in the Louvre, which is presumably an intentional joke as well as a convenient classical model.[16] In the 1799 Knole inventory both Locatelli's bust and statue of La Baccelli were, hardly surprisingly after Dorset's marriage, recorded as having been banished to storerooms.[17]

The third Duke was an aficionado of billiards, tennis and cricket as well as of women: 'What is human life but a game of cricket and, if so, why should not the ladies play it as well as we?'[18] As ambassador, he even tried to convert the French to the game. He held a match in the Champs-Élysées in 1786 and on arrival at Dover in 1789 – having been recalled from Paris, where he was briefly succeeded by Earl Gower, the future Marquess of Stafford and Duke of Sutherland – he had to stop his team from embarking for

In August 1799, a few weeks after Dorset's death, an inventory of the contents of Knole was taken by Thomas and James Clout and the future author of the 1817 guidebook, John Bridgman.[27] In the Cartoon Gallery, so-called because of its early 17th-century full-sized oil copies of the Raphael Cartoons, they catalogued:

A Canopy of State of crimson silk damask wrought and fring'd with gold/ A Chair and 3 Stools of the same/ A platform to dit[to] covered with crimson Cloth.[28]

This must have been the ambassadorial state canopy (Sackville Collection; Fig. 3), which had accompanied Dorset to France with its chair and stools *en suite* (the footstool and platform have disappeared). British ambassadors were entitled to an official equipage, including a canopy and tester (in this case embroidered in high relief with the royal arms), as well as a chair of state, two stools, a footstool and a state portrait of the king or, as became customary, of both the king and queen. In 1985 Martin Drury published both Dorset's and Whitworth's ambassadorial furniture, which are recorded in the Lord Chamberlain's accounts.[29] Like the second Earl of Buckinghamshire's state canopy at Blickling, Norfolk, made for his embassy to Catherine the Great of Russia (1762–65), Dorset's canopy was subsequently converted into a four-post bed, which by 1864 was in the 'Canopy' bedroom.[30] Remnants of Whitworth's state canopy also survive.[31] The full-length portraits of George III and Queen Charlotte, which would have hung on either side of the duke's canopy,[32] were one of 153 pairs made in Allan Ramsay's studio,[33] albeit particularly good ones, retaining their original carved and gilded frames.[34] In accordance with standard procedure, Dorset also received an allowance for silver to entertain diplomatic guests. In April 1784, he acquired an exceptionally large and elaborate service, engraved with the royal arms and the Garter, from Jeffrey and Jones, Goldsmiths and Jewellers of Cockspur Street, near Charing Cross, which included 12 dozen plates for the sum of £2,463 17s 7d.[35]

Dorset's high-backed chair of state and flanking stools (Fig. 4) may have been made not for him but for the short-lived preceding embassy in 1783 of George Montagu, fourth Duke of Manchester.[36] This set, like Whitworth's, was supplied by John Russell (c. 1773–1822), chairmaker to King George III, and on the inner face of the seat rail of the chair is the ink signature 'Fryer July 1783', who was presumably one of his craftsmen.[37] The cabriole-legged chair and stools are distinctly *retardataire* in design, but plain walnut furniture appears to have been the standard for ambassadors at the time. Indeed, the archaic appearance of Dorset's chair of state, and others similar, reflected the traditional design of contemporary state furniture, supplied under the Lord Chamberlain's aegis, including the gilded royal thrones.[38] Ambassadorial sobriety was not to the taste of George Hervey, 2nd Earl of Bristol, ambassador to Spain, who, in 1758, tried to prevent the Lord Chamberlain's department from sending him:

> the wood work of the great chair, of the two stools and the foot stool that are plac'd under the State, for I perceive they are plain frames, and as I propose setting up more ornamental ones…but I wou'd have the damask with the gold fringe belonging to it sent for the covering of the chair and stools I intend making here [in Madrid].[39]

On his return from Paris to London, the third duke married and settled into unwonted domesticity, taking care to preserve the antiquity of Knole, for which he was congratulated by Edmund Burke, who declared that he 'would not change Knole…for all the foppish structures of this enlightened age'.[40] Although he was even richer (his wife brought him an extra £13,000 p.a.), his last years were beset

by increasing melancholy and parsimony. Initially all went to plan: three children were born between 1792 and 1795, and his London house at 33 Grosvenor Square was done up by Richard Tait (fl. 1786–1827), upholder, cabinetmaker and undertaker, of 92 Jermyn Street, London.[41] Tait is known to have supplied furniture in 1794 to St. James's Palace for the apartments of Prince Edward, Duke of Kent,[42] and his accounts for Dorset show that his services even embraced, 'throwing the Snow off the House' on 13 February 1795 and on 4 June 'illuminating the front of the house with colour Lamps' for a party.[43] He revamped the 'Nursery's' for Dorset's children, fitted up the dining room with new mahogany furniture, including a sideboard, two pedestals and 30 'very large and strong Mahogany chairs,

FIG 3 State canopy turned into four-post bed, 1783, John Russell (c. 1773–1822), silk damask and embroidery, 316 x 183.6 x 214.7cm, Knole, Kent (Sackville Collection) Photo: Ben Blossom, 2016

FIG 4 Chair of state and stools, 1783, John Russell, carved and polished walnut and beech upholstered in crimson silk damask, 129.5 x 74 x 61cm (chair); 56 x 61 x 48cm (stools), Knole, Kent Photo: Ben Blossom, 2016

3

4

with 3 Splatts in the back…cover'd with fine red morocco leather'.[44] The window curtains were of 'rich strip'd sattin'.[45] He repaired, enlarged and gilded picture frames, and on 17 December 1796 hung '6 pictures in Dining and Anti-rooms'.[46] In May 1797 the dining room hang was enhanced by 'the picture by Guido [Reni]', which Tait fitted into its 'very large picture frame' that had already been altered by 'enlarging all the members & adding others, richly carved, & gilding the whole in burnish'd gold' at a cost of £45 10s.[47] He also sent men to fetch other pictures from Orton, a house near Peterborough, which were 'to come to London' in packing cases. Tait charged 3s 6d on 13 February 1795 'To putting handles into 2 Foxes tails to Brush pictures'. The duke is known to have cared for his pictures. Four of the best, including Reni's *Lucretia*, were covered with green curtains as a protection against light and dust.[48] Tait's account, from 24 February 1795 to 31 December 1797, amounted to a total of £5,255 13s 11¾d. He was not paid in full and was forced to address his concerns to the duch-ess on 16 January 1799 (the duke was to die on 19 July that year), stating that 'the things that I have had the honour of supplying are the best that can be made & are charg'd at a fair price.'[49] Tait had worked also at Knole and Stoneland, Sussex, which was also inventoried in 1799 after the duke's death.

The Reni, the only picture described specifically by Tait, was presumably the whole-length *Lucretia*, acquired by Dorset in Rome in 1771, and inherited by the Earls of Plymouth via Dorset's daughter, Mary. It was sold at Christie's in 1955, and is a high-quality copy after the prime version of 1626, which since 1769 has been at the Neues Palais in Potsdam.[50] Dorset's preference for carved and gilded frames of high quality, mainly in standard patterns, both for Old Masters and for the portraits and subject pictures that he commissioned from Reynolds, Gainsborough, Nathaniel Dance and other contemporary artists, can be deduced from the pictures remaining at Knole which were bought in Rome, Venice and London from 1770 onwards. The precisely carved frame of Ugolino (1773), in matt and burnished oil and water gilding, is typical of these, being of Maratta type.[51] The neoclas-sical frame of the large *Finding of Moses* by Luca Giordano (1634–1705; Sackville Col-lection) is the most unusual of his frames.[52] The picture was 'Bought by His Grace in London' in 1775 for £175. Its frame, presum-ably made in London about the same time, consists of an inner moulding of lotus leaves reversing at the circular boss at the centre of each section, framed with egg and dart, with a reeded and ribboned outer moulding (Fig. 5). Carved elements are missing at all four corners, but were clearly intended to be rams' heads.[53] Rather odd to our eyes now is the duke's choice of a carved giltwood Maratta frame, also London-made, for what was then regarded as 'A portrait of Raphael by Raphael', painted on panel (Sackville Collection), which

the duke bought in Venice in April 1771. A more elaborate Italianate frame of Maratta section, but highly decorated and finely carved, houses *Judith with the Head of Holofernes* by the Ferrarese painter Garofalo (1481–1559), which the duke bought in London in 1775 for £25. Four watercolours by Charles-Louis Clérisseau (1721–1820) of Roman ruins, listed among the 1770 Roman purchases as costing £33 12s, are in delicate frames of pierced giltwood revealing black stained wood beneath.

A second set of ambassadorial furniture at Knole (Fig. 6) was listed in the 1864 inventory:

> A large carved state Gilt Chair/with stuffed seat back and elbows covered with rich crimson watered silk and finished with gold color braid/ A 19 in Gilt foot stool with stuffed top and covered en suite/ A pair of 24 in Ottoman stools with stuffed tops ensuite & covered in crimson silk to match./ N.B. The above State Chair and 3 stools were used by Lord Whitworth when Ambas-sador at Paris.[54]

This set was supplied in 1802 to Whitworth by the same Russell workshop, which had made the third duke's ambassadorial furniture.[55] The chair and the stools are markedly Grecian, based on the sabre-legged *klismos*. Without the account in the Lord Chamberlain's ledgers specifically describing a 'large Grecian Elbow state chair frame' and its matching stools, one might have imagined that they were of a later period and possibly intended for Whitworth's 1813–17 term of office in Dublin, as sug-gested by the 1906 Knole guidebook, which describes 'the state chairs of Lord Whitworth when Viceroy of Ireland'.[56] No record has been found of a new set being

FIG 5 Section of frame surrounding *The Finding of Moses* by Luca Giordano (1634–1705), carved and gilt wood, 198 x 272cm (picture); 228 x 302 x 10.5cm (frame) Knole, Kent (Sackville Collection) Photo: Ben Blossom, 2016

made for the Irish embassy, so the 1802 set may have been used on both occasions. That Russell produced an up-to-date style of chair for Whitworth's embassy is evident by comparison to contemporary Parisian seat furniture.[57] A comparable, though not identical sabre-legged state chair (supplied by Russell for the trial of Queen Caroline) is at Grimsthorpe Castle and two similar chairs of state were recently on the art market: one formerly belonging to Lord Stuart de Rothesay, ambassador to France in 1815-24 and 1828-30.[58] Whitworth's ambassadorial portraits of King George III and Queen Charlotte remain at Knole in massive frames, surmounted by crowns, which were supplied by William Adair, the royal carver and gilder, whose label survives on the back of the frame of the king's portrait.[59]

After postings to Poland and Russia, Charles, Lord Whitworth, who had been Dorset's right-hand man in Paris at the outset of his embassy in 1783 – was briefly ambassador to the First Consul, Napoleon Bonaparte, during the Peace of Amiens (1802–03). According to Talleyrand, his mission was:

…suivre les Negotiations qui doivent completter l'heureux retablissement de la paix entre la Republique francaise [sic] et le Royaume uni [to follow the negotiations which must complete the happy re-establishment of peace between the French Republic and the United Kingdom].[60]

Peace was not to last long, but as long as it did, the English flocked to Paris. Whitworth was appointed on 10 September 1802, arrived in the French capital on 16 November and was presented to Napoleon, as First Consul, on 7 December. His wife, Arabella, Duchess of Dorset, was received by Josephine Bonaparte, the future Empress, at St Cloud on 11 December 1802. Arabella's portrait by Elisabeth Vigée-Lebrun, which is signed and dated May 1803, was finished just in time for their enforced return to London when diplomatic relations between Britain and France were severed on 12 May 1803 and Britain declared war on 18 May. Despite being praised by Napoleon as a '*fort bel homme*' (like his predecessor, the third duke, Whitworth was extremely handsome) he was eventually famously snubbed and the renewed conflict culminated in 1815 at Waterloo.

We are much better informed about Whitworth's acquisitions and living arrangements in Paris than Dorset's. On 19 April 1802, François Benois, from 1804 the Prince Regent's confectioner, who later acted for him in the purchase of works of art in Paris,[61] wrote to Whitworth in London, informing him that the 1720s hôtel de Charost on the Faubourg Saint-Honoré had been leased as his embassy for 6,075 livres or 6,000 francs a month.[62] The same contract reveals that the house was partially furnished.[63] Benois announced that in a few days he and '*le valet de chambre tappissier*' [who would have been involved in providing furnishing textiles, but a *tapissier* also arranged pictures and presumably other objects] would move in so that all could be made ready for the ambassador's arrival.[64] This may have been M. Guibert, who undertook and commissioned work and signed off several bills. One bill for painting furniture, partly in the '*Chambre a couché [sic]*' and '*Boudoir*' of '*madame*

6

la duchesse', notes that the work was done '*sous les ordres du citoyen Guibert tapissier*'.[65] Benois and the *tapissier* prepared the apartments both for Whitworth and for his suite, as well as the kitchens and offices. He had found '*une très belle batterie de cuisine complete, qui conviendra parfaitment a milord*' [a very beautiful complete set of copper pots and pans, which will suit your Lordship perfectly].[66] The hôtel de Charost is near the hôtel d'Évreux, now better known as the palais de l'Elysée, the seat of the French president. After Whitworth's departure, the house was sold to Napoleon's sister, Princess Pauline Borghese, from whom it was acquired by the Duke of Wellington in 1814. It has been the British embassy ever since.[67]

Despite the relative urgency with which Whitworth and the duchess had to leave Paris in May 1803, great care was taken in packing up the contents of the embassy and shipping them to Knole. The papers which chart the departure of Whitworth's belongings are detailed enough to form a picture of his way of life in the French capital. Benois was involved once again, but one of the two inventories was drawn up by an intriguing figure in the art world of post-Revolutionary France. Geoffrey de Bellaigue's pioneering 1968 article on Martin-Eloi Lignereux (1750/51–1809), '*marchand de curiosités*', marchand-mercier, furniture designer and cabinetmaker, mentions his employment by Whitworth, noting that his services extended to 'that of fine-art packer!'[68] His premises at rue Vivienne 44, near the Palais Royal, were extremely popular with English travellers during the Peace of Amiens. The preparations for Whitworth's departure were recorded in his journal by one of Lignereux's English customers, who noted that 'the buzz of War is everywhere' and that the ambassador's departure for London marked 'the first public avowal of hostility'.[69]

Lignereux's inventory – and the almost identical version by François Benois, which also lists the contents of other cases not packed by Lignereux – provide substantial information about Whitworth's Parisian establishment and both will be published, with other relevant documents, by the present authors in a subsequent article.[70] There is only space

FIG 6 Chair of state and stools, 1802, John Russell, carved and gilt beech upholstered in crimson silk, 122 x 80 x 68.5 (chair); 55 x 60 x 56.5cm (stool); 28 x 50 x 46cm (footstool), Knole, Kent
Photo. © National Trust/
Charles Thomas

here for a summary of their contents. Although it is surprising to find someone as celebrated as Lignereux packing up a household, this doubtless had much to do with Lignereux's English courtly connections. He himself had been in London in early 1802, where his late business partner, Dominique Daguerre (d. 1797), had played an important role in the furnishing of the Prince Regent's palace, Carlton House.[71] The shipment consisted of 234 cases containing a household miscellany including gilt bronzes, clocks, ornaments, porcelain, furniture, textiles, books and engravings, carriage and harness, kitchen copperware and other hardware, table and wearing linen, mirrors and silverware, as well as 2,400 litres of wine. These were all to be conveyed via Calais to Dover.

The most imposing single object, still identifiable at Knole, is a late Louis XIV Boulle clock of around 1710, on a later pedestal of around 1780 (Fig. 11) with a movement signed, on an enamel oval within a gilt bronze sunflower, by '*Etienne Baillon Paris*' for Étienne Baillon (1677–before 1748).[72] It is described precisely in Lignereux's and Benois's inventories, as being packed in four crates: the top ('*Le haut de la pendule de boullè*') was in crate 86; the base ('*le bas de la pendule boullè*') was in crate 89; the finial ('*Un enfant qui fait le couronnement de la pendule de boullè*') was in crate 190; and the barometer ('*un Barometre pour la pendule de Boulle*') was in crate 191.[73] The clock's gilt bronze mounts – elaborate in design yet fairly crude in execution – are centred upon a youthful Louis XIV, who sits enthroned, flanked by two pairs of seated female figures, the pair below personifying Fame and the Arts. Above is an obelisk-shaped barometer, with white enamel plaques marked '*PLUVIEUX*', '*CHANGEANT*' and '*BEAUTÉ*', the lower half in the form of a royal canopy, the upper part decorated with the radiant Apollo mask of the Sun King flanked by putti. This splendid creation was thought by the 1864 inventory taker at Knole to have been 'presented to Lord Whitworth by Louis

XVI'. Although Lignereux sold antiques to his clients, he was not the vendor. A sales invoice reveals that '*Une Grande Pendule de boule dont les bronzes Réprésentent [sic] Louis 14 prix fait. 900 [francs]*' was acquired by Whitworth from Jacob Frères on 11 May 1803.[74] Jacob also charged 110 francs for repairs. The pedestal incorporates Boulle marquetry, in a rather different taste, partly on a red ground (unlike the clock case), which suggests that the marriage between the clock/barometer and the pedestal was arranged later, possibly in the last years of the reign of Louis XVI.

A large library desk or *bureau plat* (Sackville Collection; Fig. 7) with three drawers of oak veneered with ebony, with gilt bronze mounts and four tapered, fluted and partly bronzed baluster legs may be the '*bureau en table en ebene garni de bronze*', listed by Lignereux in crate 87, and possibly the '*1 Table de Bureaux garni de bronze doré 320 fr*', supplied, with other furniture, by Chaudesaigues, '*M[archan] de de Meubles*' of 89, rue St Honoré.[75] The table was in the Library at Knole by 1864, when it was described as: 'A 6ft: 3 Ebony Writing Table with 3 drawers richly mounted in Ormolu [.] Top covered in green morocco leather'.[76] The original writing surface, framed in gilt bronze, is of green leather, with a neoclassical gilt border, incorporating running acanthus and anthemions. The desk probably dates from around 1780-90 and is eclectically inspired by the furniture of André-Charles Boulle, by 1760s *goût grec* and late 18th-century design. Its distinctive frieze mounts comprise bosses in square framed compartments above the legs, with a medallion-shaped central lock flanked by running acanthus and bell-flowers on the central drawer front, while the two flanking drawer front panels contain a vigorous running guilloche pattern. The side friezes follow a similar arrangement, with, in the centre, a head of Bacchus, which derive from early 18th-century Boulle equivalents, flanked by panels ornamented with guilloche. The distinctive legs, with gilt bronze laurel-leaf *chandelles* between the flutes and with inverted arrow-feather foot mounts terminating in circular ribbed roundels, are reminiscent of furniture stamped by, or attributed to, Joseph Baumhauer (*marchand ébéniste privilégié du roi suivant la cour*; c. 1749–72) and Philippe-Claude Montigny (1734–1800).[77] The closest equivalent is a graceful *bureau plat* (complete with its *cartonnier*) of slighter proportions, attributed to Joseph, which shares with the Knole desk the layout of the long and short friezes and the tapering gilt-bronze mounted fluted legs (in this case with Ionic capitals).[78]

An elegant centre table at Knole (Figs. 8a & 8b) incorporating 17th-century Boulle marquetry but with neoclassical mounts may be the table packed in crate 68, identified as '*une table en marqueterie de boulle*'.[79] The panel of the top, with its symmetrical design of grotesques and arabesques intertwined in a complex structure of scrolls and flowers and surmounted by a pierced overarching *treillage* cupola, is reminiscent of engravings by Boulle's contemporary, Jean Berain the Elder (1640–1711).[80]

FIG 7 Library table, *c.* 1780–90, Paris, ebony with gilt-bronze mounts, 81.5 x 189.4 x 96.5cm, Knole, Kent (Sackville Collection)
Photo: Ben Blossom, 2016

8a

8b

The stretcher and frieze is veneered with other reclaimed Boulle veneers. The tapered legs have capitals in the form of lotus leaves, with anthemion mounts above, similar to those on the documented pair of cabinets by Lignereux in the Royal Collection.[81]

In 1987, Christie's sold from Knole, on behalf of the Trustees of the Knole Estates, a small bureau and *gradin* (a separate drawer section on the desk top) with extremely extravagant and idiosyncratic polychrome chinoiserie Boulle, mother-of-pearl marquetry and gilt-bronze mounts, which was then identified as the table in crate no. 68 (Fig. 9).[82] However, the table just described is a more likely candidate because the 1803 Whitworth inventory is very specific in its descriptions, clearly distinguishing between tables, desks, *encoignures* (corner cupboards) and other types of furniture. Christie's put forward a tentative suggestion that the small desk might be from Germany, which seems likely, given that polychrome Boulle and mother-of-pearl furniture was particularly popular at the South German

and Prussian courts.[83] Indeed, Frederick the Great's mother, Queen Sophie Dorothea, owned a small polychrome chinoiserie turtle shell, brass and mother-of-pearl inlaid bureau with marquetry similar in style to the Knole one. It was destroyed during the War at Schloss Monbijou, Berlin.[84] The marquetry of the ex-Knole and Monbijou desks are related to the series of similar pieces of furniture in polychrome Boulle marquetry and mother-of-pearl attributed to the Maître du Bureau de l'Électeur,[85] but they are *sui generis* and clearly by another unknown, most probably German, cabinetmaker. The naturalistic and highly chased mounts also suggest a German origin. Christie's also noted another similar example, almost identical to the ex-Knole desk, attributing it to the same maker.[86]

Whitworth's imports from France also included seat furniture and cushions transported in crates 72–75 and 78–81.[87] This upholstered Directoire furniture (Fig. 10), of mahogany with discreet gilt-bronze ornaments, of which two sabre-legged sofas survive at Knole (Sackville Collection), was covered in pale blue silk damask with velvet borders in 1864, and has convincingly been ascribed to Georges Jacob, whose son had married Lignereux's daughter in 1798.[88] Documentary evidence suggests that Whitworth acquired directly from Jacob a set which had been made for another customer '*Monsieur Trudaine*'.[89]

Finally, crates 20 and 21 contained the two sections of a clock incorporating a two-horsed chariot in the case-work ('*Cage de la pendule a chare a deux chevaux*' and '*Pendule a chare, deux chevaux*') and another made of biscuit porcelain (both presumably lost and not listed in the 1864 Knole inventory); and a third with a figure of Omphale, wife of Hercules, which was listed in 1864 and is still at Knole (Sackville Collection; Fig. 1).[90] It is likely to be the clock acquired by Whitworth from G. Jacques of 6, rue du Temple, whose bill shows that he sold '*une pendule a figure dite Omphalle [sic]*' at a cost of 850 livres less a reduction of 50, so 800 livres.[91] The case is entirely of burnished gilt bronze. Omphale, Queen of Lydia, sits on the dial case, draped with a Herculean lion pelt, holding her husband's club in her left hand. The relief panel on the front, framed with oak leaves, alluding to Hercules's heroic wreath, depicts the god in Omphale's thrall, holding a distaff, flanked by heads of Hercules. At least one other model has appeared on the art

FIGS 8a & 8b Centre table, *c.* 1800, incorporating Boulle marquetry and gilt-bronze mounts, 77.3 x 101 x 53.6cm, Knole, Kent
Photo: Ben Blossom, 2016

9

FIG 9 Bureau formerly at Knole and sold by Christie's London in 1987, *c.* 1720, German(?), polychrome marquetry and gilt-bronze mounts, 125 x 89.5 x 52.5cm
Photo: © Christie's Images Ltd 2016

10

FIG 10 Pair of Directoire
armchairs formerly at Knole
and sold at Christie's London
in 1988, *c.* 1790–1800, Georges
Jacob (1739–1814) and sons
Photo: © Christie's Image's
Ltd 2016

market.[92] The movement has been replaced by one signed
on the white enamel dial 'Barwise & Son's', whose premises
were at 29 St Martin's Lane and who by about 1805 were
watch and clock makers to the Duke of Cumberland and
by 1820 to George IV.[93]

Whitworth is known to have had a penchant for Empire
clocks, one of which, sold from Knole and acquired in 1996
by the Rijksmuseum,[94] may be the '*pendule à étude*' supplied
for 700 livres (including a reduction of 20 livres), also by
G. Jacques.[95] It is dominated by a patinated bronze draped
female figure personifying Study, leaning on a draped
giltbronze pedestal piled with books that incorporates the
clock dial. The mahogany-cased base is decorated with a
gilt-bronze relief of putti in various 'learned' poses. This may
well be the clock listed in the library of Whitworth's house
at 45 Grosvenor Place, London.[96] The Rijksmuseum clock
has a movement by Vulliamy, the firm that replaced the
movements of most of the Prince Regent's French clocks,
and Whitworth certainly employed the Vulliamys in 1811.[97]
A gilt-bronze Parisian wall or cartel clock of around 1750,
elaborately carved with flowers, birds, oak leaves, crossed
quivers and arrows and surmounted by a Cupid (Sackville
Collection), may well have been a Whitworth purchase as
it has a Vulliamy dial and movement, while retaining its
elaborate gilt-bronze hands. A pair of four-light gilt-bronze
wall sconces in the form of baskets of flowers upheld by
decorative ropes and ties is about the same date as the cupid
clock (Sackville Collection).

Another magnificent clock at Knole takes the form of
a patinated figure of Virgil with a gilded bust of Homer
on a gilded plinth (Sackville Collection; Fig. 12). The dial
is signed '*L. Ravrio Bronzier à Paris*' for Louis-Stanislas
Lenoir-Ravrio (1783–1846), the son and successor, in 1814,
of Antoine-André Ravrio (1759–1814). A more symmetrical variant of the clock exists, where the bust is flanked by
Virgil and a female representation of Poetry.[98] The early
versions of the clock, completed between 1805 and 1814
by Ravrio, were made with a marble base and gilt-bronze
ornaments, while the one at Knole is entirely of gilt and
patinated bronze. All versions incorporate a bas relief
representing Virgil reading the *Aeneid* to Augustus and
Livia. Augustus's sister, Octavia, faints when she hears the

verses alluding to the premature death of her son Marcellus.
This clock must have been acquired during Whitworth's last
two visits to Paris in April and October 1819. Indeed, that
caveat applies to everything at Knole that is not specifically
mentioned in the 1802–03 documents.

When the Whitworths went to Ireland as Viceroy and
Vicereine in 1813 on the princely salary of £30,000 p.a., the
summit of Whitworth's diplomatic career was darkened by
the accidental death of the young fourth Duke of Dorset in
an Irish hunting accident in 1815. Both Whitworth and the
Duchess died in 1825. The 1864 Knole inventory reveals
that their presence was still felt in the house. As well as the
furniture described here, 'Lord Whitworth's dress Court
Suit' was in the King's Bedroom, while his 'Coronation
Robe…Dress Sword and a silver Coronet' were also listed.
Although the claim that much of the French furniture was
'presented to Lord Whitworth by the Emperor Napoleon
the first' cannot be substantiated, its connection with the
Peace of Amiens is of considerable interest. Together with
the purchases made by the third Duke of Dorset during his
previous embassy to the doomed court of Louis XVI, this
furniture bears witness to a distinguished episode in the
long history of Knole.

*Christopher Rowell is Furniture Curator of the National
Trust and Chairman of the Furniture History Society.*

*Wolf Burchard is the National Trust's Furniture Research
Curator.*

ACKNOWLEDGEMENTS
The authors are grateful above all to
Lord Sackville for giving them
permission to study the private
collection and archive and to publish
documentary material and
photographs. His kindness and that of
The Hon. Mrs. Hugh (Bridget)
Sackville-West, as well as their advice
and help, have been fundamental to
the preparation of this article. We are
also grateful to Emma Slocombe,
National Trust curator responsible for
Knole, and to Helen Fawbert and her
colleagues there, for their continual
assistance and the provision of
information. Specialist advice on
aspects of the collection has been
provided by Reinier Baarsen, Rufus
Bird, John Chu, Peter Hughes and Sir
Hugh Roberts.

1. For the Gole table see: Gervase
Jackson-Stops, 'A Courtier's
Collection – The 6th Earl of Dorset's
Furniture at Knole I', *Country Life*, vol.
CL, no. 4170, 2 June 1977, p. 1496; Th.
H. Lunsingh Scheurleer, 'Pierre Gole,
Ébéniste du roi Louis XIV', *The
Burlington Magazine*, vol. CXXII,
June 1980, p. 386 and *Pierre Gole:
Ébéniste de Louis XIV*, Dijon, 2005,
pp. 168–72; Christopher Rowell in
Michael Snodin and Nigel Llewellyn
(eds.), *Baroque: Style in the Age of
Magnificence* (exh. cat., The Victoria
and Albert Museum, London),
London, 2009, p. 349, cat. 140;
Whitworth is called Earl Whitworth
here, even though he did not receive
the earldom until 1815. He was

elevated to the Irish peerage in 1800,
so throughout the Peace of Amiens,
he was Baron Whitworth.
2. For a general account of Knole and
of the period under discussion here,
see Robert Sackville-West, *Knole,
Kent*, London, 1998 (2003 ed.),
especially pp. 80–85.
3. For recent literature on Knole's
upholstered royal furniture, with
further references, see: Emma
Slocombe, 'Ancient Furnishing: The
Display and Alteration of Upholstered
Seat Furniture and Textiles associated
with the Brown Gallery, Knole, in the
Nineteenth Century', *Furniture
History*, vol. L, 2014, pp. 297–325;
Olivia Fryman, *Making the Bed: The
Practice, Role and Significance of
Housekeeping in the Royal Bedchambers
at Hampton Court Palace, 1689–1737*,
PhD thesis, Kingston University, 2011
and 'Rich Pickings: The Royal Bed as
a Perquisite, 1660-1760', *Furniture
History*, vol. L, 2014, pp. 119–36;
Christopher Rowell, 'The King's Bed
and its Furniture at Knole', *Apollo*, vol.
CLX, November 2004, pp. 58–65 and
'A Set of Early Seventeenth-Century
Crimson Velvet Seat Furniture at
Knole: New Light on the 'Knole Sofa'
Furniture History, vol. XLII, 2006,
pp. 27–52.
4. Svend Eriksen, *Louis Delanois:
menuisier en siège (1731–1792)*, Paris,
1968, pp. 52–53; 'Le Comte Dorset'
was probably the title that he had
assumed by courtesy as the heir to his
uncle, the second duke, who died in
1769. Had the second duke had a son

himself, he would doubtless have been called Earl of Middlesex, the title borne by the second duke before succeeding to the dukedom.

5. Christopher Rowell, Alastair Laing and James Rothwell, 'Acquisitions 2004–06' in *The National Trust Historic Houses and Collections Annual 2006*, published by Apollo, p. 40.

6. Michael Hall, 'French Porcelain at Knole: The 3rd Duke of Dorset's Sèvres Collection', *Apollo*, vol. CXXXIX, May, 1994, pp. 38–42.

7. Ann Bramley, 'A duke on Grand Tour: John Frederick Sackville, 3rd Duke of Dorset', *The British Art Journal*, vol. VII, no. 2 (Autumn 2006), pp. 75–81 and John Ingamells, *A Dictionary of British and Irish Travellers in Italy, 1701-1800*, New Haven and London, 1997, p. 306.

8. Kent History and Library Centre, Maidstone (henceforth KHLC), U269/E416.

9. Payments to Reynolds as recorded in the duke's list of purchases sometimes differ from the charges entered in Reynolds's own ledgers, see John Coleman, 'Reynolds at Knole', *Apollo*, vol. CXLIII, April, 1996, pp. 24–30; for the portrait see: David Mannings and Martin Postle, *Sir Joshua Reynolds: A Complete Catalogue of His Paintings*, New Haven and London, 2000, vol. I, p. 403, no. 1568 and John Chu, 'High Art and High Stakes: The 3rd Duke of Dorset's Gamble on Reynolds', *British Art Studies 2*, http://dx.doi.org/10.17658/issn.2058-5462/issue-02/jchu

10. Vials himself described the frame as 'broad bold rich burnish gold whole length frame, carved with knull and hollows, rich foliage, leaf and stick'; see Jacob Simon, 'A Guide to Picture Frames at Knole', Kent: http://www.npg.org.uk/research/programmes/the-art-of-the-picture-frame/guides-knole.php; for Thomas Vials, see 'British picture framemakers, 1600-1950': http://www.npg.org.uk/research/conservation/directory-of-british-framemakers/v.php

11. Robert Sackville-West, *Inheritance: The Story of Knole and the Sackvilles*, London, 2010 (paperback edn., 2011), p. 132.

12. Ibid., p. 133.

13. The attribution to Locatelli is due to the late Rupert Gunnis; see the entry on Locatelli in Ingrid Roscoe, Emma Hardy and M.G. Sullivan (eds.), *A Biographical Dictionary of Sculptors in Britain 1660–1851*, New Haven and London, 2009, pp. 742–44.

14. Ibid., pp. 742–43.

15. Sackville-West 2011, p. 132.

16. The duke may well have seen the Hermaphrodite – dug up in 1608 and restored in 1619, when the mattress was added by Bernini – in the Borghese collection in Rome.

17. The bust was in the Wardrobe and the statue was at the 'Top of the Stairs next the Wardrobe'.

18. Quoted in Gerald M. D. Howat, 'Sackville, John Frederick, third duke of Dorset (1745–1799)', *Oxford Dictionary of National Biography*, Oxford University Press, 2004; online

edn, Jan 2008 [http://www.oxforddnb.com.ezproxy2.londonlibrary.co.uk/view/article/24445, accessed 17 April 2016] from Arthur Haygarth (ed.), *Frederick Lillywhite's cricket scores and biographies from 1746-1826*, vol. I, 1862.

19. Howat 2004, online edition 2008, quoting Elizabeth Einberg, *Gainsborough's 'Giovanna Baccelli'*, London, 1976, p. 11.

20. Quoted from *Prophecies delivered by a descendant from the Oracle of Delphos of the future lives and deaths of the following distinguished personages*, Dublin, 1791, in Sackville-West 2011, p. 134.

21. Howat 2004, online edn., 2008.

22. Wilmarth Sheldon Lewis (ed.), *The Yale Edition of Horace Walpole's Correspondence*, New Haven and London, 1971, vol. XXV, p. 487 (Walpole to Horace Mann, 30 March 1784).

23. KHLC, U269/A243/13.

24. Howat 2004, online edn. January 2008.

25. Sackville-West 2011, p. 134.

26. David Peters, *Sèvres Plates and Services of the 18th Century*, London, 2005, cat. no. 84–13, pp. 729–30.

27. KHLC, U69/E5: 'An inventory Of all the Pictures, Statues, Busts, Household Goods & Furniture At Knole in the County of Kent. Directed by the last Will and Testament of the late Duke of Dorset. To be considered as Heir Looms Taken the 12th. &c. of August 1799 by Thomas Clout & John Bridgman & James Clout'. This inventory includes 'Mr Bridgman's Room', so perhaps he was on the staff at Knole.

28. Ibid.

29. Martin Drury, 'Two Georgian Chairs of State and a State Canopy at Knole', *Furniture History*, vol. XXI, 1985, pp. 243–49.

30. Ibid, p. 244, 248 and 249, figs. 5 and 6; another example of a canopy of state (1761), from the House of Lords, being converted into a bed is at Grimsthorpe Castle, see Hugh Roberts, 'Royal Thrones, 1760–1840', *Furniture History*, vol. XXV, 1989, pp. 61–85, fig. 9.

31. We are grateful to Emma Slocombe for confirming this and to Zenzie Tinker for sending photographs.

32. A single portrait of the reigning monarch was usually hung within the state canopy against the tester, but Dorset's canopy tester incorporates raised work depicting the royal arms, so his pair of portraits of George III and Queen Charlotte must therefore have hung on either side of the canopy.

33. Oliver Millar, *The Later Georgian Pictures in the Collection of Her Majesty The Queen*, London, 1969, pp. 93–95, no. 996.

34. The Knole Ramsays retain their original frames, of an enriched Maratta type, surmounted by crossed laurel branches and crowns. They are attributed to Isaac Gosset and dated 1784 (payment to Ramsay was made belatedly in 1785); see Jacob Simon, 'Frame Studies: II Allan Ramsay and

Picture Frames', *The Burlington Magazine*, vol. CXXXVI, no. 1096, July, 1994, p. 452, fig. 65.

35. KHLC, U269/A243/14. On 4 June 1796, '5 large plate chests' at Dorset House, Whitehall were repaired by Richard Tait, during his refurbishing of the interior for the third duke in the mid 1790s (Sackville Collection, Knole).

36. Drury, op. cit., p. 244.

37. Ibid., pp. 244 & 247, fig. 2.

38. Roberts 1989, pp. 62–66 and figs. 1–8.

39. National Archives, SP 94/252 Spain, supplementary 1755-60, f188: The second Earl of Bristol to J. Richardson [chief clerk in the Southern Department, Whitehall], Madrid, 16 Oct 1758. Rec 6th November. Bristol had moved directly from Turin to Madrid. His silver and much of his furniture bought abroad is still in the collection at Ickworth, Suffolk (NT). We are very grateful to James Rothwell for sharing this reference with us. It will be cited at full length in his forthcoming *Courtly Entertaining: The Ickworth Silver*, to be published in 2016 by the National Trust and Philip Wilson Publishers.

40. Quoted in Sackville-West, 2010 (paperback edn. 2011), p. 127.

41. For the houses in Grosvenor Square, see F.H.W. Sheppard (ed.), *Survey of London*, vol. XL, *The Grosvenor Estate in Mayfair, Part 2 (The Buildings)*, London, 1980, pp. 117–66.

42. Geoffrey Beard and Christopher Gilbert (eds.), *Dictionary of English Furniture Makers, 1660–1840*, Leeds, 1986, p. 870.

43. Sackville Collection, Knole; the illumination of the house cost four guineas; for the history of such illuminations, see Melanie Doderer-Winkler, *Magnificent Entertainments: Temporary Architecture for Georgian Festivals*, New Haven and London, 2013.

44. Sackville Collection, Knole.

45. Ibid.

46. Ibid.

47. Ibid.

48. Bramley 2006, pp. 78–79.

49. Ibid.

50. Stephen Pepper, *Guido Reni: L'Opera Completa*, Novara, 1988, pp. 260–61, no. 97, copy no. 3, where described as a studio copy of high quality (228.6 x 160cm). It was sold at Christie's on 22 July 1955, lot 79 and reappeared at Sotheby's, 25 November 1970, lot 65, since when it has been several times on the art market.

51. Nicholas Penny, 'Frame Studies: I. Reynolds and Picture Frames', *The Burlington Magazine*, vol. CXXVIII, no. 1004, November, 1986, p. 819 and fig. 39.

52. John Bridgman, *An Historical and Topographical Sketch of Knole in Kent; with a brief Genealogy of the Sackville Family Embellished with Engravings*, London, 1817, p. 16. The Giordano then hung in the Hall.

53. We are grateful to Bridget Sackville-West for this information, which was first noticed by Francis

11

FIG 11 Late Louis XIV Boulle clock, *c.* 1710, on a later pedestal of *c.* 1780, and with a movement by Étienne Baillon (1677–before 1748), Boulle marquetry and gilt-bronze mounts, 138 x 70 x 35cm, Knole, Kent
Photo: Cecilia Divizia, 2016

FIG 12 Mantel clock with figure of Virgil and bust of Homer, *c.* 1819, Louis-Stanislas Lenoir-Ravrio (1783–1846), gilt and patinated bronze, 68 x 44.4 x 17.9cm, Knole, Kent (Sackville Collection)
Photo: Ben Blossom, 2016

12

Russell, who pointed out that an identical frame for a Marieschi of *St Mark's, Venice*, was sold at Christie's, 13 December, 1996, lot 78 and that *The Music Lesson* by Gaspare Traversi (Nelson-Atkins Museum F61–70) also has the same pattern of frame.

54. KHLC, U269/E6: 'The Following The Inventory of Sundry Personal Effects made Heirlooms, at Knole, Sevenoaks, Kent; The Property of Mary Sackville, Dowager Countess Amherst Deceased. Taken September 1864. William Aspinwall Valuer &c. 70 Grosvenor Street London'.

55. Drury, op. cit., p. 245.

56. National Archives, Lord Chamberlain's Accounts, LC11/8: 'Ambassador to France / To a large state canopy frame with cover and/cornices Prepared for carving and loose mouldings/ lay on to the directions of the Upholsterer, [£]9. 5[s] / To 1 large Grecian Elbow state chair frame/ high back shaped feet and elbows neatly carved/ and prepared for gilding and stuf[f]ing [£]5 8[s] / To 2 high stools to match the chair @ 8/(?) [£]5 16[s]// To 1 D[itt]o footstool d[itt]o d[itt]o [£]1 10[s]'; and Lionel Sackville-West [third Lord Sackville], *Knole House: Its State Rooms, Pictures and Antiquities*, Sevenoaks, 1906, p. 26.

57. A very similar 'Directoire' armchair by Georges Jacob is illustrated in Pierre Kjellberg, *Le Mobilier Français du XVIIIe Siècle: Dictionnaire des ébénistes et des menuisiers*, Paris, 2002, p. 467.

58. Bonhams, London, 21 November 2012, lot 157; and Sotheby's, London, 10 July 1998, lot 99; and for Grimsthorpe Castle see Roberts 1989, p. 68, fig. 13.

59. Jacob Simon, 'A Guide to Picture Frames at Knole', Kent: http://www.npg.org.uk/research/programmes/the-art-of-the-picture-frame/guides-knole.php; for William Adair, see 'British picture framemakers, 1600–1950': http://www.npg.org.uk/research/conservation/directory-of-british-framemakers/v.php

60. This letter from Talleyrand in the Sackville Collection, Knole, was actually addressed to the Marquess Cornwallis, who signed the Treaty of Amiens on behalf of the United Kingdom on 25 March 1802, but Talleyrand's definition of the aim of the British embassy was still accurate when Whitworth arrived. Cornwallis must have handed over this correspondence to Whitworth, hence its survival among the family papers at Knole.

61. His documented visits to Paris in 1815, 1817 and 1820 and his purchases on behalf of the Prince are recorded in *Carlton House: The Past Glories of George IV's Palace*, exh. cat. (The Queen's Gallery, Buckingham Palace), London, 1991. He certainly worked for the Prince as early as 1804 (information from Rufus Bird) and continued to be employed both as cook and as art scout during his reign as George IV; see also Geoffrey de Bellaigue, *French Porcelain in the Collection of Her Majesty The Queen*,

3 vols, London, 2009, vol. I, p. 11.

62. These figures derive from an anonymous note headed 'Payements faits [sic] pour mylord Whitworth', KHLC, U269/O211.

63. KHLC, U269/O210: 'Lists, bills, letters concerning hire of a house in Paris for Lord Whitworth, transportation of baggage between England and France and inventories of household goods, 1802–03.'

64. At the Salon (the annual exhibition of pictures at the Louvre) a member of the Académie royale de Peinture et de Sculpture was responsible for the arrangement; see for example, Ryan White, 'Exhibiting Enlightenment: Chardin as *tapissier*', *Eighteenth-Century Studies*, vol. XLVI, no. 4, Summer 2013, pp. 531–54.

65. KHLC, U269/O211, 'Mémoire des meubles lésivé [sic] & Repeint a neuf pour son Excelance [sic] L'ambassadeur D'angletaire [sic]'. The bill was submitted by Mouginot of 308, Faubourg St Germain, who received 177. 10 livres.

66. KHLC, U269/O210.

67. Mary Beal and John Cornforth, *British Embassy, Paris: The House and its Works of Art*, London, 1992, p. 4 and Tim Knox, *The British Ambassador's Residence in Paris*, Paris, 2011, p. 37.

68. Geoffroy [sic] de Bellaigue, 'Martin-Eloy Lignereux and England', *Gazette des Beaux-Arts* (May–June 1968), vol. LXXI, p. 293; Lignereux was described in the *Almanach du commerce de Paris pour l'An IX* [1800/1801] as 'marchand de curiosités'.

69. J.P.T. Bury and J.C. Barry (eds.), *An Englishman in Paris: 1803. The Journal of Bertie Greatheed*, London, 1953, p. 137 and 148. Greatheed (1759–1823) was a gentleman poet and playwright, who was accompanied by his eponymous son, who was a copyist and portrait-painter.

70. Both KHLC U269/O210; Christopher Rowell and Wolf Burchard, 'François Benois, Martin-Eloi Lignereux and Lord Whitworth: Leasing, Furnishing and Dismantling the British Embassy in Paris during the Peace of Amiens, 1802-3', *Furniture History*, vol. LII, 2016 (forthcoming).

71. De Bellaigue 1968, p. 283. Daguerre had a shop in London (1786–96); for Daguerre and Carlton House, see Carlton House, op. cit., p. 11 and *passim*.

72. Étienne Baillon was the son of Jean-Baptiste I Baillon, a clockmaker from Rouen. He was apprentice to Isaac and Jacques Thuret at the Galeries du Louvre in the immediate vicinity of André-Charles Boulle's workshops, and married the grand-daughter of the Gobelins painter Jean-Baptiste Monnoyer. He was first established in rue des Orties (1708) and later in the Rue de Richelieu (1714); see Jean-Dominique Augarde, *Les Ouvriers du Temps : La Pendule à Paris de Louis XIV à Napoléon Ier/ Ornamental Clocks and Clockmakers in Eighteenth Century Paris*, Geneva, 1996, p. 272.

73. KHLC, U269/O210: 'Estas du contenut [sic] des caisses de M. l'Ambassadeur', undated but certainly late May or early June 1803.

74. KHLC, U269/O211: 'Facture de Meubles fournis a Son Excellence Lord W[h]itworth par Jacob freres ébénistes Rue Meslée No. 77' [23 Floréal XI (11 May 1803, not 23 April 1803, as stated in a later note in pencil on the upper left corner of the sheet)].

75. Christie's King Street, 17 June 1987, lot 73, p. 142; the relevant document is in KHLC, U269/O211.

76. KHLC, U269/E6.

77. A *bureau plat* with similar legs, ascribed to Montigny, is illustrated in Kjellberg, 2002, p. 634, fig. a.

78. Alexandre Pradère, *French Furniture Makers: the Art of the Ébéniste from Louis XIV to the Revolution*, London, 1989, fig. 246, p. 240, formerly 'owned by Lord Malmesbury [the 1st Earl, a distinguished diplomat] who bought it in 1796', and sold Sotheby's Monaco, June 1981, lot 144, of a type of which two were listed in Joseph's posthumous inventory after 1772. Another smaller centre table, stamped Joseph, c.1770, has very similar legs to the Knole desk; see Ibid., fig. 245, p. 240.

79. KHLC, U269/O210.

80. Compare: *100 planches principales de l'œuvre complet de Jean Bérain, 1649–1711*, Paris (undated, probably 1882) and Jérôme de La Gorce, *Berain: Dessinateur de Roi Soleil*, Paris, 1986.

81. RCIN 31308; see De Bellaigue 1968, pp. 286–88 and figs. 4–5; Hugh Roberts, *For The King's Pleasure: The Furnishing and Decoration of George IV's Apartments at Windsor Castle*, London, 2001, pp. 150 and 163, fig. 190; and Christopher Rowell, 'French Furniture at Uppark: Sir Harry Fetherstonhaugh and his Friends in Post-Revolutionary Paris', *Furniture History*, vol. XLIII, 2007, pp. 271–72, fig. 3.

82. Christie's King Street, 17 June 1987, lot 73, pp. 140–42; the authors are very grateful to Adam Kulewicz, Christie's, for providing them with the relevant information regarding this sale, which 'paid for the restoration of the park at Knole after the devastating storm of 1987', Sackville-West 2010 (paperback edn. 2011), p. 148.

83. Ibid., p. 141.

84. Thomas Kemper, *Schloss Monbijou: Von der königlichen Residenz zum Hohenzollern-Museum*, Berlin, 2005, figs. 266–67, pp. 264–65.

85. For a full account of this series, see Christopher Rowell, 'A Louis XIV Polychrome Boulle Marquetry Bureau by the '*Maître du Bureau de l'Électeur*' at Saltram', *Furniture History*, vol. XLVII, 2011, pp. 19–46.

86. Christie's King Street, 18 June 1987, lot. 73, p. 141; the relevant piece of furniture is reproduced – attributed to Domenico Cucci – in Helena Hayward (ed.), *World Furniture*, 1965, colour plate facing p. 97. It was then in the Lopez-Wilshaw Collection.

87. KHLC, U269/O210.

88. Eight sabre-legged armchairs and two *bergères* (from a different set with turned legs) were sold at Christie's, London on 23 June 1988, lots 78 and 79. The two sabre-legged sofas remain at Knole (Sackville Collection). The 1864 inventory describes the covers as 'pale blue satin damask with rich cut Genoa Velvet borders'; for the union between the Jacob and Lignereux families, see Jean-Pierre Samoyault, 'The Jacob Lignereux Alliance (14 March 1798)', *Furniture History*, vol. XLIII, 2007, pp. 20–28.

89. Christie's King Street, 18 June 1987, lot. 79, referring to KHLC, U269/O211: 'Bills for purchases made in France while Ambassador'.

90. KHLC, U269/O210 (op. cit): no. 20: *Cage de la pendule à chare [sic] à deux chevaux / Cage de la pendule Omphale / Cage de la pendule de biscuit; no. 21: Pendule à chare [sic] à deux chevaux / Pendule biscuit / Pendule Omphale* and the 1864 inventory, KHLC, U269/E6.

91. KHLC, U269/O211 (op. cit.): '*Note des objets déposé[s] chez L'ambassadeur d'Angleterre par Moi G. Jacques Manufactures de Bronze dores rue du Temple*' [undated but almost certainly early 1803].

92. With The Three Centuries Shop, Vancouver, Canada, in 2016.

93. A.D. Stewart, 'Barwise & Sons watchmakers to the King. A brief history of family and firm', *Antiquarian Horology* (March 2014), pp. 621–34.

94. Reinier Baarsen, *Paris, 1650–1900: Decorative Arts in the Rijksmuseum*, New Haven and London, 2013, pp. 458-9, no. 113.

95. KHLC, U269/O210.

96. Baarsen 2013, p. 459, where the undated inventory is stated to be among the Sackville MSS at the KHLC, U269/E149.

97. Ibid.

98. Marie-France Dupuy-Baylet, 'L'Énéide' (vers 1805) in *Pendules du Mobilier national, 1800–1870*, Dijon, 2006, p. 64-65.

UN ALLER-RETOUR POUR KNOLE

THOMAS GAINSBOROUGH'S PORTRAIT OF LOUIS-PIERRE, MARQUIS DE CHAMPCENETZ

Gainsborough's fine portrait of the marquis de Champcenetz is returning to Knole this year. JOHN CHU explains how the French nobleman, a friend of John Frederick Sackville, third Duke of Dorset, found shelter in England in turbulent times

THIS YEAR SEES the permanent return to Knole of one of the most beautiful and stylish portraits ever to hang on its walls: Thomas Gainsborough's painting of the French nobleman Louis-Pierre Quentin de Richebourg, marquis de Champcenetz (1754–1822) (Fig. 1). Having formed part of the collection since at least 1793, when it was in the possession of the sitter's friend John Frederick Sackville, third Duke of Dorset, the painting was sold in 1930 to a collector in the United States, where it remained, in several different hands, until its reappearance for sale at Sotheby's in New York this January and its acquisition for Knole.[1]

In some ways, the portrait is composed much like any other bust-length likeness of an 18th-century gentleman – compare it, for example, to Joshua Reynolds' portrait of the third duke (Fig. 2). Yet this compositional simplicity belies the brilliance with which Gainsborough brings Champcenetz to life. The way the sitter ever so slightly inclines his head and meets the viewer's gaze out of the corner of his eye creates, with great nuance, the impression of a fleeting encounter. It is an ingeniously captured moment of intimate recognition.

No less evocative of the sitter's lively presence is the picture's virtuosic brushwork. The basic brown 'ground' layer of paint, upon which the rest of the picture is built up, is left visible at multiple points beneath the exceptional thinness of Gainsborough's application, especially in the white 'stock' that winds around Champcenetz's neck, the shadow of his cheek and his powdered hair or wig. 'Reserving the ground' in this way is an economical way of creating a mid tone, but when done with finesse, as here, it also serves to enliven the picture with a glowing, inner warmth. The highlights and shadows of the features have been achieved through the delicate flickering of a fine brush across the smooth pink and white flesh tones. More boldly, the burst of snowy linen and ivory silk on the marquis's chest is formed of a remarkable flurry of wet-on-wet brushstrokes, the varying thinness and dryness of which conjure up the complex folding and twisting of fine textile. The 1839 guidebook to Knole summed up this captivating mixture of simplicity and artistic facility appositely when it described the piece as an 'unassuming, but most clever picture'.[2]

On stylistic grounds the portrait is dated to the early to mid 1780s, when the sitter was about thirty years old and Gainsbor-

ough was in his late fifties and at the height of his powers. He attracted a number of French sitters around this time, painting portraits of the dancer Gaëtan Vestris (now in a private collection), his son Auguste (now in the Tate) and the soprano Madame Lebrun (now in the Art Gallery of South Australia). This dating is consistent with the period when the third Duke of Dorset was acquiring works from the painter for his houses on a lavish scale. A leading collector of modern British art (and never one to skimp on the finer things in life), the duke also purchased three landscapes by Gainsborough, two bust-length portraits of himself and a 'fancy picture' of the soprano Elizabeth Linley and her brother, the composer Thomas Linley, in the guise of rustic gypsies (Fig. 3). Most eye-catchingly, he also commissioned a dazzling full-length portrait of his mistress, the opera dancer Giovanna Baccelli, mid-performance, in full stage costume and make-up. This work was exhibited at the Royal Academy in 1782 (Fig. 4).

The sitter is first identified as the 'Marquis Champcenitz' in the 1799 posthumous inventory of the third duke's heirlooms.[3] However, the earliest documented record of the picture at Knole is in the 1793 edition of a popular guidebook, *The Ambulator: or, a Pocket Companion in a Tour Round London, within the Circuit of Twenty Five Miles*.[4] The picture is identified with the simple description 'a French Nobleman, Gainsborough', and is listed as hanging in the Blue Room. This comfortable chamber was part of a suite of fine ground-floor apartments opening onto the gardens. Dorset for the most part lived in this suite, away from the venerable splendours of the state rooms above.

The Blue Room, named after the colour of its damask upholsteries, was densely hung with pictures. The works were chosen both to uphold its status as a ducal dwelling and to reflect its domestic use by the family. Champcenetz, therefore, could be seen alongside paintings attributed to Raphael, Correggio and Rembrandt, whose works the duke had been collecting since his succession in 1769. Champcenetz also shared wall space with Gainsborough's picture of the Linley siblings and portraits of personal significance to the Sackvilles, including two drawings of Dorset's wife, Arabella, by Nathaniel Dance and a miniature of his grandfather, Lionel, first Duke of Dorset.[5] It was not unusual for Dorset, here and elsewhere, to display old and new paintings, British and foreign works, or portraits and subject pictures alongside each other. Nevertheless, it is worth noting that the portrait of Champcenetz hung in a room characterised by a sense of luxury, cosmopolitanism and familial intimacy.[6]

Significantly, a miniature of Louis XVI by Louis-Marie Sicard, dated 1785, was also displayed in this room, along with a further portrait of that king and his wife, Marie Antoinette, painted on Sèvres porcelain.[7] The third Duke of Dorset was British ambassador to the court of Versailles between 1784 and 1789, during which period he developed a particularly close attachment to Marie Antoinette (he continued to supply her with English gloves after his return to England).[8] As Christopher Rowell and Wolf Burchard discuss elsewhere in this magazine (see pp. 42–52), in this respect, the third duke followed in the Sackville family tradition of maintaining close links to centres of

FIG 4 *Giovanna Baccelli,* 1782, Thomas Gainsborough, oil on canvas, 226.7 x 148.6cm, Tate, London

European power, especially the royal court of France. His involvement in the politics and culture of that nation surely helped to bring him into orbit with Champcenetz and to nurture their friendship.

Champcenetz was born on 22 September 1754 to Jean-Louis, marquis de Champcenetz, and his first wife, Marie-Rose Teissier. He descended from a Breton family of courtier-civil servants (a group known in France as the *noblesse de robe*) and was himself involved with the ruling Bourbon dynasty throughout his career.[9] Unlike their counterparts in Britain, in France the eldest sons of certain nobles were permitted to assume their fathers' titles during their lifetimes. Until the death of Jean-Louis in 1813, therefore, Jean-Pierre was officially known as the marquis de Champcenetz, le fils. Also available to him were his father's lucrative positions in the royal household. By 1776, when he was 22, he was already the *gouverneur*, or official overseer, of the palace of Meudon and captain of the hunt for the same estate *en survivance* (by inherited right).[10] Jean-Pierre also followed in the family tradition of consolidating official duties with bonds of friendship with the royal family, becoming the particular favourite in youth of the comte d'Artois, youngest brother of Louis XVI.

By the time he was painted by Gainsborough, Champcenetz had seen notable action in the field of battle. Beginning as *sous-lieutenant* to the Mestre-de-Camp-Général-dragons at the age of 16, he rose quickly over the course of the 1770s through the dragoons to attain the rank of *capitaine*. It was only at the end of the decade, however, when France entered into open hostilities with Britain in the American War of Independence, that real opportunities for active service arose. Supporting rebels in Britain's North American colonies as aide-de-camp to maréchal Charles du Houx de Vioménil, he faced down 'innumerable dangers', including several confrontations with British forces and a bout of the plague.[11] Off the coast of Long Island on 5 September 1782, for example, he 'spirited' the crew of the *Aigle* with 'courage and great valour' during the frigate's two-day engagement with the mighty *Hector*, a 74-gun British ship of the line.[12] Later that month, when the *Aigle* ran aground in the Delaware River with an entire British squadron bearing down on it, the captain of the ship, the comte de la Touche, ordered:

M. de Champcenetz to throw himself, with the American Pilots and some sailors, into the only boat that remained; and,

as soon as the boat had got clear off, l'Aigle struck her colours. The English frigate in the meanwhile observing the boat rowing away, directed its whole fire at it. The pilot in the utmost alarm wished to surrender, but M. de Champcenetz, with sword in hand, compelled them to sustain a shower of balls, and to pass up the river.[13]

There is good reason to think that this intrepid wartime adversary was in fact something of an enthusiast for Britain. Champcenetz, after all, was born into a Parisian milieu that was gripped by a remarkable *anglomanie* that only increased over the course of the 1770s and 1780s. This current of French high culture manifested itself in many ways during these decades, ranging from fads for typically English forms of dress to the circulation of serious philosophical texts applauding the political structures of France's more 'liberal' neighbour.[14] Champcenetz was certainly 'perfectly acquainted with the English language' by the time of the war because he acted as translator between the captain of the *Aigle* and her American pilots.[15] Moreover, he was already friends with the third Duke of Dorset by the turn of 1778, from which time we have a bill for Dorset from a quality Parisian gunmaker, delivered care of Champcenetz (Figs. 5 & 6). In fact, the two were sufficiently close for the marquis to pay half the balance in livres on the duke's behalf.

By the 1780s, Champcenetz was moving in the circles of the richest and most prominent *anglomane* in France, Louis Philippe, duc d'Orléans (1747–93). In this decade, Louis Philippe granted Champcenetz the rank of *mestre-de-camp* in the Orléans-dragons against the express wish of Marie Antoinette, flouting the tradition of giving such high positions to members of the older *noblesse d'épée*.[16] Orléans was so enamoured of his ideal of the private English gentleman that he made regular visits with his entourage to London, taking the lease on a Robert Adam mansion in Portland Place and sitting for Sir Joshua Reynolds (Fig. 7).[17] Befriending George, Prince of Wales, and other leaders of English high society, he also followed the fashionable round to Brighton, York races and so on. Champcenetz certainly joined Orléans in England during his temporary exile from France in 1789–90, although there were plenty of earlier visits during which he could have joined the prince in London and sat for Gainsborough, who had died by the time of this last visit.[18] The Prince of Wales observed to his brother Frederick in the midst of Orléans's first exhausting stay in May 1783 that the:

town is at present much enliven'd by ye. arrival of ye. Duc de Chartres [Louis Philippe's title until 1785] & a large party of French both men & women, who thank God are going away next week … My reason for saying I was glad ye. French were going, is not because I disliked ym. but because we have had so many parties & fêtes & assemblies & suppers upon their account, yt. Everybody is grown quite tired of ym.[19]

Notwithstanding the extravagant lifestyle of the French in London in the 1780s, the elegant simplicity of Champ-

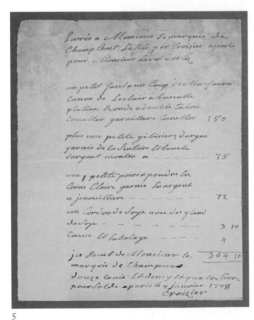

5

6

FIG 7 *Louis-Philippe, duc d'Orléans*, 1786, John Raphael Smith (1752–1812) after Joshua Reynolds, mezzotint, 65.3 x 45.2cm, Nunnington Hall, Yorkshire
Photo: © National Trust/Robert Thrift

with distinction in war. This vision of cosmopolitan manliness evidently appealed to the third duke and perhaps even served to mirror his own ideal self-image.[23] In the 19th century, however, this picture had a quite different significance. It served as a reminder of the devastating events in which Champcenetz found himself caught up.

In John Bridgman's *Historical and Topographical Sketch of Knole* of 1817 (by which time the picture had been moved upstairs to the Venetian Dressing Room), the entry on Gainsborough's *Monsieur Campchinetze* is accompanied by the following biographical note, outlining the sitter's desperate escape to England after the bloody storming of the Tuileries Palace by Revolutionary forces on 10 August 1792 (Fig. 9):

> He was an officer of the Swiss guards when they were overpowered by the furious Jacobins in the Thuilleries, at the commencement of the French Revolution; and lay some hours concealed amongst the dead soldiers, till night afforded him an opportunity to escape. Being conversant in the English language, he passed himself for a native of that country, and quitted Paris in the disguise of a servant. He lived for some time as an ostler at an inn on the road, till at length he was so fortunate as to escape to England, where he resided many years. He frequently visited the Duke of Dorset both in London and Knole.[24]

This is the first and shortest of several accounts published over the course of the 19th century of this most dramatic phase of Champcenetz's life. The marquis was, of course, not a Swiss Guard but rather *gouverneur* of the palace, having assumed the role after his father fled for Italy at the start of the Revolution. He did, however, act as personal attendant and bodyguard to the royal family until its flight from the palace. The remainder of this version of events broadly accords with those that followed, the 'ostler at an inn' episode excepted.

A biography published in 1831 of William Huskisson, who was secretary to Earl Gower, the British ambassador in Paris, in 1792 informs us that, after extricating himself from the palace, having 'either been thrown, or ... jumped from, one of the windows', Champcenetz 'contrived with much difficulty to make his way unperceived to the hotel [townhouse] of the British Ambassador; where, by passing

FIG 8 Coat, waistcoat and breeches, *c.* 1780, France, wool, lined with silk and linen, with cut steel buttons, Victoria and Albert Museum, London

cenetz's costume in the Gainsborough portrait, not least his blue tailcoat, may very well be a deliberate signal of the sitter's *anglomanie*. The adoption of English customs by French aristocrats carried a hint of rebelliousness against the obligations and prohibitions that their own court imposed on them. If the newfound passion for the relaxed sociability of tea parties and horse racing was an expression of longing for the more independent lives of their English counterparts, the plain, close-cut tailcoat – always worn with dashing riding boots – became a veritable Anglophile uniform.[20]

Quite distinct from the brightly coloured and highly embroidered French silk suits, which, in *ancien régime* France, it was the nobleman's patriotic duty to don, a pocketless navy blue *justaucorps* with narrow tails and turn-down collar known as a *frac* (after 'frock coat') spoke of fashionable sporting pursuits and the longed-for freedoms of a country estate.[21] Outfits of this kind were by no means simple and inexpensive. In the Victoria and Albert Museum there is an English-style suit of the 1780s made of such fine broadcloth that, during recent conservation, only its lavish white silk lining required extensive attention (Fig. 8). Similarly, while Champcenetz's waistcoat is unembellished, matching the colour of his shirt in understated fashion, it is evidently made of silk. Champcenetz's spick and span blue tailcoat, meanwhile, is distinctive for the stylish and practical feature of an additional button-down thong on each side of the lapel, presumably designed to keep the turn-down collar neatly in place during country walks, hunting parties and riding expeditions.[22]

Gainsborough's portrait captures a gallant young chevalier in his prime – a fashionable man of the world who enjoyed a raft of connections and inherited privileges yet had nonetheless survived hardship and acquitted himself

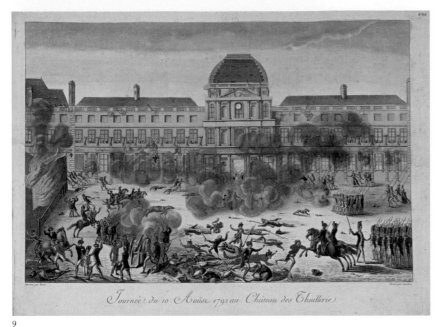

9

FIG 9 *Journée du 10 Août 1792
au Château des Thuillerie*, 1792,
Madame Jourdan after G. Texier,
tinted etching, 36 x 52cm,
Bibliothèque nationale
de France, Paris

himself for an Englishman, he had obtained access to the
apartments of Mr Huskisson, with whom he was slightly
acquainted.'[25] Fearing that harbouring one 'so closely
attached to the Royal Family' might cause a diplomatic
incident, yet determined not to turn Champcenetz over
to 'the blood-thirsty populace', Huskisson 'furnished him
with money and whatever else he required' and entrusted
him to 'the protection of a laundress, on whose fidelity he
knew he could confide'.[26]

Grace Dalrymple Elliott (Fig. 10), the British mistress
of Orléans, who had herself been painted by Gainsborough in the 1780s, takes up the story.[27] Having been
mysteriously summoned to Paris from her Meudon estate,
Elliott conveyed Champcenetz, by then stricken with
fever, to her Parisian townhouse under cover of darkness,
braving a citywide manhunt for the marquis and other
aristocratic escapees of the Tuileries massacre.[28] Since
warrants to search the houses of Champcenetz's associates
had been issued, Elliott found that the only possible place
to secrete the marquis was in her own chamber, between
the mattresses of her bed and the wall. When the National
Guards searched her house, only the courtesy of the com-
manding officer prevented her from being removed from
her bed by a rabble of soldiers and stopped Champcenetz
from being discovered.[29]

Having quietly nursed her protégé to a better state of
health, Elliott marshalled the reluctant assistance of Orléans, now hailed as Philippe Égalité and the figurehead of
a powerful Revolutionary faction, to smuggle the marquis
to the port of Boulogne and thence to the safety of England. There he remained until the Bourbon restoration of
1814, maintaining his friendship with the Duke of Dorset.
Once back in Paris, he married Armande-Pauline-Marie
de Castellane and resumed his duties as *gouverneur* of the
Tuileries until his death on 4 May 1822. He is buried in
the cemetery of Père Lachaise.

Notwithstanding some rather inventive variations
on the spelling of his name, Louis-Pierre, marquis de
Champcenetz, le fils, continued to be identified at Knole
as the sitter in Gainsborough's portrait throughout the
19th and early 20th centuries. As the picture migrated

from the Venetian Dressing Room to the Crimson Drawing Room (or the Reynolds Room), and thence to the
Music Room, successive Knole guidebooks maintained
this identification.[30]

It was only on the eve of the picture's sale in 1930
that confusion set in over exactly which member of
the Quentin de Rochebourg family was represented.
In his *History of the Sackville Family* (1927), Charles
J. Phillips mistakenly attributed the slanderous publication *Petit traité de l'amour des femmes pour les sots*
to the marquis.[31] The work was in fact penned by his
younger half-brother, the satirist Louis-Edmond (b.
1760), who in 1794 lost his head on the guillotine for
his anti-Revolutionary writings.[32] When the picture
was catalogued in 1972, by which time it formed part
of the Kimbell Art Museum collection in Texas, the
entry on the picture provided the name and biography of Louis-Edmond, but with the title 'chevalier de
Champcenetz', which actually belonged to another
younger half-brother, René-Ferdinand (1762–1849).[33]
When the picture went up for sale in 2016, its title had
become a conflation of these younger brothers' names,
and was sold under the description 'Portrait of Louis-
René Ferdinand Quentin de Richebourg, Chevalier de
Champcenetz'.

The return of this portrait to Knole has allowed us to
establish the correct identity of the sitter and to trace the
major events of his life. Perhaps fittingly, the travels of the
portrait – from London, where it was painted, to Knole,
where it resided for over 130 years, to North America via
Paris, and then back to Knole again – have uncannily mir-
rored those of Champcenetz himself.[34] There is still much
to discover about Louis-Pierre, marquis de Champcenetz,
not least concerning his visits to London during Gainsborough's lifetime. Yet for now, we can rest assured that
his portrait has returned permanently to a place where
he found refuge and the solace of friendship in times of
international turmoil.

*John Chu is Assistant Curator of Pictures and Sculpture at
the National Trust.*

ACKNOWLEDGEMENTS
Many thanks to Amanda Bradley,
Wolf Burchard, Katie Scott, Nicole
Ryder, David Pullins, Christine
Sitwell and David Taylor for
discussing this article and the portrait
of Champcenetz with me. I am
particularly grateful to Emile de
Bruijn, Sarah Grant, and Emma
Slocombe for providing invaluable
leads for research.
1. The picture was sold by
Major-General Sir Charles
Sackville-West, fourth Lord Sackville
(1870–1962), via Spink, London, and
Jacques Seligmann & Co., New York,
to the stockbroker and collector André
de Coppet of New York (1892–1953)
for £5,000. It then passed through the
Newhouse Galleries, New York,
before entering the collection of Mr
and Mrs Kay Kimbell of Fort Worth,
Texas, whence it passed into The
Kimbell Art Museum. It was sold at

Sotheby's in London on 12 July 1989
(lot 38) to A. Alfred Taubman. The
National Trust acquired the picture at
the sale of Taubman's old-master
paintings at Sotheby's in New York on
26 January 2016 (lot 61).
2. John H. Brady, *The Visitor's Guide to
Knole*, London, 1839, p. 134.
3. KHLC, U269/E5, 'A Copy of the
Inventory of all the Pictures, Statues,
Busts, Household Goods & Furniture
at Knole, Directed by the Will of the
Late Duke of Dorset to be left as Heir
Looms. Taken by Thomas Clout, John
Bridgman & James Clout. August 12
&c. 1799'. The picture is recorded in
the Organ Room in this document.
4. *The Ambulator: or, a Pocket
Companion in a Tour Round London,
within the Circuit of Twenty Five Miles*,
London, 1793, p. 161.
5. KHLC, 1799 Knole Inventory
(see footnote 3).
6. For an overview of the 1799

10

Léonard Cobiant.

30. The portrait is recorded as being in the Blue Room in successive editions of the *Ambulator* between 1793 and 1800, although it is listed as being in the Organ Room in the 1799 inventory of heirlooms. From the time of the publication of *An Historical and Topographical Sketch of Knole* in 1817 until about 1896, the picture was in the Venetian Dressing Room. A green pencil note, probably inscribed in 1896, in the 'Inventory of Sundry Personal Effects…of Mary Sackville, Dowager Countess Amherst, Deceased' (September 1864), places the picture in the Crimson Drawing Room (now the Reynolds Room), 1864 Knole Inventory, Sackville Collection. By 1906, it had moved to the Music Room. See Lionel Sackville-West, *Knole House: Its State Rooms, Pictures and Antiquities*, Sevenoaks, 1906, p. 88.
31. Phillips, op. cit., vol. II, p. 251.
32. Prévost and d'Amat, op. cit., p. 313.
33. *Kimbell Art Museum: Catalogue of the Collection*, Fort Worth, 1972.
34. The stretcher and the back of the painting (which has been relined) bear French customs stamps that date from its passage via Paris from Knole to New York in 1930.

hanging scheme that notes the mix of old-master and contemporary pictures, see Francis Russell, 'Picture Hanging at Knole in 1799', *Apollo*, March 1989, pp. 168–72.
7. KHLC, 1799 Knole Inventory (see footnote 3).
8. Charles J. Phillips, *History of the Sackville Family*, 2 vols., London, 1927, vol. II, p. 248.
9. M. Prévost and Roman d'Amat (eds.), *Dictionnaire de biographie française, tome 8*, Paris, 1959, p. 312.
10. M. de la Chenaye-Desbois, *Dictionnaire de la Noblesse, tome 11*, Paris, 1776, p. 620.
11. Louis Philippe, comte de Ségur, *Memoirs and Recollections of Count Segur*, London, 1825, pp. 322, 400.
12. 'French Gazette on the Engagement with the Hector of 74 guns', *The Political Magazine and Parliamentary, Naval, Military, and Literary Journal*, July 1782, p. 690.
13. Ségur, op. cit., p. 322.
14. See Josephine Grieder, *Anglomania in France, 1740-1789: Fact, Fiction, and Political Discourse*, Geneva, 1985 and Derek Jarrett, *The Begetters of Revolution: England's Involvement with France, 1759–1789*, London, 1973, pp. 183–216.
15. Ségur, op. cit., p. 321.
16. Grace Dalrymple Elliott, *Journal of my Life During the French Revolution*, London, 1859, pp. 101–02; Prévost & d'Amat, op. cit., p. 312.
17. See especially Évelyne Lever, *Philippe Égalité*, Paris, 1996, pp. 207–31 and Philip Mansel, 'Courts in exile: Bourbons and Orléans in London, from George III to Edward VII' in Debra Kelly and Martyn Cornick (eds.), *A History of the French in London: Liberty, Equality, Opportunity*, Oxford, 2013, pp. 102–03.
18. See the letter of Joseph Hyacinthe François de Paul de Rigaud, comte de Vaudreuil, to Charles Philippe, comte d'Artois, written on 17 January 1790: '[Champcenetz] après avoir dîner à Londres avec M. le duc d'Orléans, il est revenue a Paris pour nuire à son père et à sa belle-mère'. Léonce Pingaud (ed.), *Correspondence intime de comte de Vaudreuil et du comte d'Artois pendent l'émigration, tome I*, Paris, 1889, p. 90.
19. *The Correspondence of George, Prince of Wales, 1770–1812*, 8 vols., London, 1963–1971, vol. I, pp. 107–108.
20. Grieder, op. cit., pp. 25–26.
21. Dominique Gaulme & François Gaulme, *Power and Style: A World History of Politics and Dress*, Paris, 2012, pp. 120–21.
22. A closely comparable buttoned-down collar features in Thomas Gainsborough's *Portrait of Lewis Bagot, Bishop of Bristol (1740–1802)* in the Birmingham Museum and Art Gallery.
23. For the third Duke of Dorset's efforts to project an image of courtly cosmopolitanism through his art collecting and other extravagant behaviours, see John Chu, 'High Art and High Stakes: The third Duke of Dorset's Gamble on Reynolds', *British Art Studies*, issue II [accessed 1 May 2016: http://dx.doi.org/10.17658/issn.2058-5462/issue-02/jchu].
24. John Bridgman, *An Historical and Topographical Sketch of Knole*, in Kent, London, 1817, p. 46.
25. John Wright, *A Biographical Memoir of the Right Honourable William Huskisson Derived from Authentic Sources*, London, 1831, pp. 22–23.
26. Ibid.
27. There is also a full-length Gainsborough portrait of Grace Dalrymple Elliott, painted in 1778, in the Metropolitan Museum of Art, New York.
28. Elliott, op. cit., pp. 71–112. The Champcenetz episode constitutes a sizeable proportion of the memoir.
29. This chain of events forms the centrepiece of *The Lady and the Duke* (2001), Éric Rohmer's film of Elliott's life during the French Revolution, in which the marquis is played by

Lady Betty Germaine's Bed Room

1

EMBROIDERED HANGINGS ON TWO BEDS AT KNOLE AND COTEHELE

The embroidered hangings in Lady Betty Germain's bedchamber did not exist during its occupant's lifetime, but were introduced in the 19th century by the Sackville family. NICOLA GENTLE examines two beds at Knole and Cotehele whose 17th-century textiles appear to have been deliberately assembled into antiquarian room-settings

FOR A LONG TIME, descriptions of the small apartment at Knole named after Lady Betty Germain (1680–1769) conveyed a romantic idea of its early 18th-century occupant (Fig. 2). In 1948, Vita Sackville-West created an image that was to persist throughout the 20th century. She describes Lady Betty as 'a somewhat prim lady' and continues: 'It is easy to picture Lady Betty stitching at the bed-curtains now hanging round her little four poster; making pot-pourri…writing many, many letters…An agreeable existence, though perhaps not a very exciting one.'[1] Two oil paintings by James Holland (1799–1870) completed in around 1845 contributed to this notion, showing female figures in early 18th-century dress engaged in leisure pursuits in Lady Betty's bedchamber.[2]

The outer hangings on what is today known as 'Lady Betty's bed' feature canvaswork embroidery, while the inner ones are of pinkish-cream quilted silk (Figs. 1 & 3).[3] Research by Emma Slocombe has revealed that the embroideries were not, however, extant in this particular room during Lady Betty's lifetime.[4] Rather, they were introduced in the 19th century, when, it appears, the Sackville family began consciously to create antiquarian settings with 17th-century textiles for those rooms at Knole open to the public.[5]

Lady Elizabeth 'Betty' Germain was the second daughter of Charles Berkeley, 2nd Earl of Berkeley. She was the second wife of Sir John Germain (1650–1718), whom she married in 1706. Her friendship with the Sackville family came about when Lionel Cranfield Sackville, first Duke of Dorset (1688–1765), married Elizabeth Colyear (1689–1768), daughter of Germain's closest friend and colleague in the Dutch service, Lieutenant General Walter Philip Colyear. From the year she was widowed until her death, Lady Betty spent much of her time at Knole in an apartment that comprised a bedchamber and a sitting room. An adjacent box room provided space for a lady's maid.

The bedchamber is first recorded in the 1730 inventory. At that time its furnishings included 'Red Silk Curtains & Counterpaine' and '2 quilts & wh. Silk quilt. 4 plumes of feathers'. The 1765 inventory lists 'one white Silk Quilt, a Carpet under the Bed, Green Silk Curtains and Counterpain'. The 1799 inventory mentions 'An oak Bedstead with crimson flowered Velvet Furniture'. It is not until 1837 that we find a description that comes close to matching the bed as it appears now: 'Oak Bedstead with Plumes, and worked stuff Furniture lined with pink & Fringed' and 'ancient Counterpane, Green Silk Counterpane, Embroider'd Counterpane, Extra'.[6]

'Worked stuff Furniture' must refer to the upper outer valances and four curtains still extant, together with a set of base valances that appear in a photograph taken in around 1865 (their current whereabouts are unknown). These hangings are decorated with linen 'slips' embroidered with wool and silk in gros point applied, with a cord gimp outlining, on to a natural linen textile. Throughout the embroidery, the imagery is predominantly foliate: an elaborate curling leaf motif with added fronds is repeated in different colourways on the valances, while the curtains display similar leaves twisting upwards around a scrolling stem that rises from a base of bare roots (Fig. 4).

Needlework slips acquired their name from gardeners' slips or cuttings: plants were often illustrated in this way in early herbals. Applied canvaswork motifs were popular during the 17th century for the embellishment of furnishings, as can be seen on the so-called Mary, Queen of Scots Bed at Hardwick Hall, Derbyshire (Fig. 5).[7] Another notable example, now in the Victoria and Albert Museum (V&A), features a row of trees, each adorned with oversized flowers (tulips and irises are recognisable). In this case, the roots are hidden in small hillocks created by chenille threads worked over padding to give a three-dimensional effect. This valance belongs to a set of bed hangings from the third quarter of the 17th century, no doubt produced a little earlier than those at Knole. Its motifs are worked in tent stitch on fine canvas applied to an ivory silk satin ground. The edges are finished with stitching in black thread rather than with a gimp.[8]

The flowering tree displaying mixed flowers, fruits and foliage on a serpentine stem is a recurrent image in English textiles of the 17th and 18th centuries. It normally appears either with its roots exposed or set on a small grassy hillock. Although most often associated with the printed cotton palampores brought from India by the East India Company, it may actually have a more complex origin. By the end of the 16th century, branched foliage decoration was already well established in English textiles, notably in black-work embroidery and needlework slips. The characteristic twisted dentate leaf may have derived from Flemish verdure tapestries, which were imported in large numbers during the 17th century, while the flowering tree with exposed roots on a rocky landscape can be traced further back, possibly to 15th-century Persian sources.[9] Elements of this ornamentation were developed and refined in England on embroidered crewelwork hangings, continuing well into the 18th century. One extant example can be found on the bed in the White Room at Cotehele, Cornwall (Fig. 6).[10]

But it is the bed hangings in another room at Cotehele that show a much closer resemblance to those at Knole (Fig. 7). The bed in the King Charles Room was supposedly slept in by Charles I in 1644 when he stopped there on his march from Liskeard to Exeter. During the 19th century, artists gave this story a romantic gloss. William James Muller (1812–45), for example, produced a sketch of the king sitting at a small table alongside the bed.[11]

Up until at least 2005, the guidebook to Cotehele stated that the King Charles Room 'is perhaps the room

2

FIG 1 Photograph of Lady Betty Germain's bedchamber, *c.* 1890, Knole, Kent
Photo: Ben Blossom, 2016

FIG 2 *Lady Elizabeth 'Betty' Germain*, 1731, Charles Philips (1708–47), oil on canvas, 40 x 29.3cm, Knole, Kent
Photo: © National Trust Images/John Hammond

3

in the house most evocative of genuine antiquity, and there is little reason to suppose that its essential furnishing has altered since its creation in the early seventeenth century.'[12] Yet 15 years earlier, John Cornforth argued that the bedrooms in this part of the house had been brought together no earlier than the 18th century as a contrived antiquarian interior. 'It is suspicious to find them set out in pairs of rooms without dressing rooms…the impression is that they were arranged to be looked at rather than slept in.' Concerning the King Charles Room, he remarked, 'The heavily carved black bed made of old woodwork has an early 19th century look. Yet it must be older, because in 1817 Charles Sandoe Gilbert wrote: "The bed furniture is of oriental workmanship hung with a deep fringe formed into knots with variegated silks."'[13] (The description of the embroidery as 'oriental' owes perhaps to its flowering-tree imagery.)

The hangings on the outside of the bed display needlework slips remarkably similar to those in Lady Betty's Room. The weave count is identical and the colour grada-

tion of silk and wool yarns is comparable, as is the gimp edging to the motifs. The use of single motifs on the valances and columns on the curtains is common to both beds, although the designs on the King Charles Room bed are larger and somewhat more elaborate, featuring floral imagery (including irises, tulips and roses) and occasionally incorporating other stitches, such as petit point and French knots. Both sets of motifs and columns are placed against an imitation of upright decorative woven lace (braid), a design device used in woven silks in the late 17th and early 18th centuries. This detail is best observed in the more sophisticated King Charles Room hangings, where the columns end with a horizontal twist of woven lace rather than the traditional hillock or bare roots (Fig. 8).

The boldness and fluidity of both designs are a departure from more static individual slips, such as those on the bed at Hardwick. No other embroideries quite resembling them are known. Could only two such sets have been made? Stylistically closest to them are the Hatton Garden hangings, produced by a professional London workshop in the second half of the 17th century and now in the V&A. These are worked as rectangular panels rather than as slips and have a wide range of stitches, including tent, cross, brick and rococo stitches, couched work and French knots. The imagery incorporates architectural features and a number of small animals, yet the foliage and flowers twisting around columns, the yarns and the weave count are comparable to those of the Knole and Cotehele hangings.[14]

At Burghley House, Lincolnshire, a large settee, mentioned in an inventory from the 1860s as being covered with antique embroidery, displays identical needlework and similar imagery – a column with trailing vines – applied to deep purple velvet. The embroidery can be traced back to 1690, appearing as item three in a schedule of household goods that had arrived from Chatsworth House, Derbyshire: 'ffour pieces of purple Velvett Hangings with Stone Worke pillars wrought in Crosse Stitch'.[15] The piece as a whole appears to be a deliberate antiquarian creation, possibly assembled for the visit of Queen Victoria in 1844.

Exact dating of the embroideries at Knole and Cotehele is difficult. In many respects, they resemble 17th-century slips, while elements of the imagery, such as the woven lace motifs, could place them in the early 18th century. There was a transition during this time from heavier, stylised floral motifs to lighter, more naturalistic forms. This can be observed in crewelwork embroidery, as well as in printed and woven textiles.[16] Incidentally, the colours and imagery of the Cotehele motifs show close parallels with those on the early 17th-century English carpet currently in Lady Betty's Room (Fig. 9).[17]

In the case of the King Charles Room hangings, the reapplication of the embroidery on to a dark brown wool jersey fabric can be traced back to the time these pieces were restored by a Mrs Breen following the National Trust's acquisition of Cotehele in 1947. The brown jersey cloth may well have been all that was available so soon after the Second World War. James Lees Milne (1908–97) related the tale in 1992:

> Then there was the bogus, highly carved Charles I bed in the last stages of decay. Should we scrap it and replace it with a spare genuine bed from another house? We decided not to. Just as someone on the estate had doubtless faked it up around 1800, so we handed it over to an incomparable jack of all trades, William Cook, who dismantled and plunged the Charles I bed into a bath of de-worming solution, having first extracted and thrown away the worst infected bits. Meanwhile we had the bed's original deep fringe with its heavy silk knots and devices, the valance and curtains re-backed and mended by an expert needle-woman, Sheila Breen, a farmer's wife on the estate.[18]

Looking at 19th-century watercolours of the room, the ground textile of the hangings appears to be a light reddish brown, while in a lithograph by Nicholas Condy (1793–1857), published in *Cotehele on the banks of the Tamar* (*c*. 1840), it appears to be green in colour. Yet the description written by the Reverend F.V.J. Arundell to accompany Condy's illustrations does indeed suggest a dark ground: 'The bed, with its massy pillars and figured back-board of very dark oak; the hangings of dark cloth, worked in silk, and its once rich coverlid, now fast falling to pieces from age.'[19] Could the 'dark cloth' have been a deep purple velvet, like that on the Chatsworth hangings at Burghley?

Mention of 'its once rich coverlid' also raises questions. In the Condy print, the coverlet appears to be of a mainly light hue, punctuated by small patches of colour. The Muller sketch and another painting suggest an overall light colour with decoration in the form of rows of triangular motifs, mostly red and blue, resembling patchwork. A patchwork quilt (*c*. 1800) is currently displayed on the bed in the neighbouring Queen Anne Room.[20] This might have been the inspiration.

The deep silk fringing retained on the outer valances of the King Charles Room bed dates from the second half of the 17th century. Its complex construction – a lattice heading with ornament of roundels and tufts and polychrome hangers – is very similar to that on the flowering-tree valance in the V&A collection already mentioned.

The hangings in the interior of the bed are made from a deep beige wool cloth, decorated with woven lace (braid) frogging, embellished with tufts and toggles, some of which could date from the 17th century. It can be deduced from their dimensions that they were originally made to hang on another bed. The bed's woodwork – some of it elaborately carved – is thought to have been assembled from various sources between the 17th and 19th centuries.[21]

The creation at Cotehele of a series of antique rooms appears to date from the 1740s, when Richard, first Baron Edgcumbe (1680–1758), inherited the house. At that time, he was beginning to modernise the principal family home of Mount Edgcumbe, Cornwall, sending the older furnishings to Cotehele – maybe because they were considered unfashionable, but perhaps also to provide a more historically resonant arrangement for the enjoyment of visitors. His third son, George, first Earl of Mount Edgcumbe (1721–95), continued this project, making Cotehele one of the earliest intentionally created antiquarian interiors.[22]

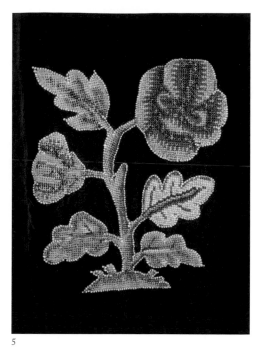

FIG 5 An embroidered slip on the so-called Mary, Queen of Scots bed at Hardwick Hall, Derbyshire
Photo: Annabel Westman

The revival of historical room-settings reached a height later in the 19th century when collectors, such as Baron Ferdinand de Rothschild at Waddesdon, employed specialist interior decoration firms to supply antique textiles made up as hangings or furniture coverings.[23] At Knole, the Sackvilles – like the Edgcumbes at Cotehele – already possessed a wealth of early furnishings and textiles with which to start creating such interiors.

The sequence of embroidered columns on Lady Betty's bed is neither regular nor symmetrical, indicating perhaps that these textiles originated in a different form. They suggest paning – the practice of alternating decorative panels with plain ones – a common feature of wall hangings of the 17th and early 18th centuries. The 1765 Knole inventory mentions 'four pieces of Cross Stitch hangings' in the 'Dutches's dressing Room', the only references to this particular embroidery technique (other than for a couple of chair covers) so far found in 18th-century listings.[24] Could this be the origin of the bed hangings?[25]

Despite the irregular placement of ornament on the curtains, the hangings have been made to sit well on the current bedstock. Matching silk fringing in sympathetic green and gold hues (possibly from the late 17th century) is deployed in the accepted manner: a deep (12cm) hanging on the upper valances; a narrower (5cm) hanging at the lower edge of the curtains and base valances; a very narrow (2cm) hanging at the top and on the side edges.[26] A double row of the narrow fringe is seamed into the central upright corners of the foot curtains. Such attention to detail could suggest this is an original construction. However, in many places the condition of

FIG 6 One of the crewelwork curtains on the bed in the White Room at Cotehele, Cornwall
Photo: the author

FIG 7 The bed in the King
Charles Room at Cotehele,
Cornwall
Photo: the author

the embroidery – in terms of wear and loss – does not correspond to that of the fringing.

When and why the base valances decorated with embroidered slips were removed is not known. It is difficult to judge their condition from the early photograph, but the 1911 inventory lists 'Bedstead with old needlework hangings and Bedding (hangings perished)'. The base valances have been replaced by sections taken from the borders of a 17th-century Indo-Portuguese quilt embroidered in chain stitch with patterning, small animals and figures. Such a quilt may have been in the collection that came to Knole from Copthall, the Essex home of Lionel Cranfield, first Earl of Middlesex, who had made his fortune trading textiles in the early 17th century and whose daughter Frances married into the Sackville family.[27]

The current inner quilted hangings, consisting of a head cloth and four valances, are less easy to identify. Their current pinkish-cream appearance might be the effect of ageing, and they may have once been white. It is possible that they came from the items mentioned in the 1730 inventory for the L.C. Baron Room: '1 Crimson Velvet Bed lined with wh. Sattin & quilted Counterpane of the Same'. (The pieces could have been taken from a counterpane.) The same inventory listed '2 quilts and wh. silk quilt' for Lady Betty's Room. The inventory of 1837 referred to 'worked stuff Furniture lined with pink & Fringed' in Lady Betty's Room, which is how the hangings appear today.

The counterpane now displayed on Lady Betty's bed is of pale green-blue silk decorated with delicate scrolling foliate embroidery and trimmed with a deep fringe, which suggests an early 18th-century origin (Fig. 4). This could be the same 'Green Silk (Curtains and) Counterpain' listed during Lady Betty's lifetime. It is depicted in the paintings of the room by Holland. The 1837 inventory lists an 'ancient Counterpane, Green Silk Counterpane, Embroider'd Counterpane, Extra'. Around the same time, a guidebook to Knole described the bedstead as antique and 'covered with two or three curiously embroidered counterpanes'.[28]

In 1906, Lionel Sackville-West described Lady Betty as 'an accomplished needlewoman' and attributed work on several chair covers, counterpanes and curtains in different parts of Knole to her.[29] So far, no firm evidence has been found to support this, although it is possible that the green silk embroidered counterpane is indeed her work. In 1763 Horace Walpole commented on the great care she gave to the fine textile furnishings she had inherited at her early marital home, Drayton House.[30] Perhaps the assumption that she did likewise at Knole has perpetuated an idealised image of her than the reality.

We now know that several items were purchased in the late 1880s to augment the room settings.[31] These include a crimson velvet bag embroidered with gold thread and a raised-work embroidered picture, both dating from the 17th century.[32] The embroidered bag was presented as Lady Betty's own and displayed alongside a spinning wheel. The raised-work picture was hung in her sitting room. Annotations on the 1864 inventory give further

evidence of pieces being moved and altered to create new furnishings around the same time:

Lady Betty Germaine's Bed Chamber 1864

A 4 ft. 3 state bedstead with Old Tapestry [pencil: 'needlework']
hanging valens and bases carved
wood vases at corners surmounted
by plumes of colored feathers.....
A Crimson and gold color silk
damask counterpane embroidered
with the Arms of The Dorset Family
This has been converted into a
Valance for Dressing room & covers to
some of the chairs in the same room

Such alterations were part of a wider scheme to change Knole's interiors during the late 19th and early 20th centuries. The introduction of embroidered textiles to this apartment in particular would have reinforced the image of Lady Betty as an accomplished needlewoman. For example, the 1911 inventory listed a 'Queen Anne stuffed over Arm Chair' with 'loose cover in old needlework' in the bedroom – a reference to the chair covered in crewelwork embroidery still displayed there today.[33] As already mentioned, by this date the bed hangings were described as 'perished'. Perhaps it was soon afterwards that the panels of early 17th-century Indo-Portuguese quilted embroidery were utilised to replace the base valances.[34]

The origin of the two similar sets of embroidered bed hangings at Knole and Cotehele may never be known. They are most likely English, dating from the late 17th or early 18th centuries (Figs. 10 & 11). Possibly professionally produced, they could have been made for wall hangings and later used to recreate the antique phenomenon of the four-poster bed.

In 1992 Lees-Milne drew parallels between the two houses:

It [Cotehele] is renowned for its contents, mostly of the seventeenth century, and may be compared to Knole in Kent, only in miniature, for

FIG 8 One of the curtains on
the King Charles bed, Cotehele,
Cornwall
Photo: the author

FIG 9 The rare 17th-century
carpet in Lady Betty Germain's
bedchamber at Knole, Kent
Photo: the author

8

9

the unusual state of its preservation, almost suspension in time, thanks largely to its isolation and ownership by one family.

The histories of both properties are currently being reassessed. It is now apparent that the impression of time suspended that Lees-Milne remarked upon resulted from the deliberate creation of antiquarian furnishings and interiors.

Nicola Gentle works as a freelance conservator and researcher of historic textiles, with a particular interest in 17th- and 18th-century furnishings.

1. Vita Sackville-West, *Knole, Kent*, London, 1948, p. 21. The same wording was still being used in the Knole guidebook of 1998. In fact, Lady Betty wrote spirited letters concerning social and political matters to the likes of Jonathan Swift.
2. One painting is in the collection at Sissinghurst Castle, Kent (NT 802394); the other is at the Yale Center for British Art (YCBA/lido-TMS-279).
3. NT 129469.
4. The current conservation project at Knole has prompted research on the history of its presentation. See Emma Slocombe, 'Never all together forgete me', *Arts Buildings and Collections Bulletin*, Winter 2014–15, pp. 15–17 and Emma Slocombe, 'Ancient Furnishing: the display and alteration of upholstered seat furniture and textiles associated with the Brown Gallery, Knole, in the nineteenth century', *Furniture History*, vol. L, 2014, pp. 297–325.
5. The first guidebook to Knole was published in 1817, when the house opened more formally to the public; these rooms were on the visitor route.
6. Kent History and Library Centre (henceforth KHLC), (number unknown), 'An Inventory of Goods at Knole Taken in Nov.r 1730', Sackville Mss. E4, 'An Inventory of Goods at Knole taken in October 1765', U269/E5. 'A Copy of the Inventory of the Pictures, Statues, Busts, Household Goods & Furniture, at Knole, Directed by the Will of the late Duke of Dorset to be left as Heir Looms. Taken by Thomas Clout, John Bridgman & James Clout. August 12 &c. 1799', Sackville Collection, '1837 Knole Inventory'.
7. NT 1127728. Individual flowers mainly stand on a small grassy mound. Weave count: 9 double picks and ends per 2 centimetres, with 9 cross stitches in both directions. The embroidery is thought to date from *c.* 1630. It has been rearranged and reapplied to black velvet at least twice in the history of the bed. Information provided by Annabel Westman.
8. Embroidered valance, V&A, T.322-1980. The museum also holds three related bed curtains, while other pieces from the set are now in the Powerhouse Museum, Sydney. The weave count of the canvas is 9 picks/9 ends per centimetre with 9 stitches per centimetre in each direction, while on the Knole bed the weave count of the canvas is 7 picks/7 ends per centimetre with 3.5 stitches per centimetre in each direction.
9. John Irwin & Katharine Brett, *Origins of Chintz*, London, 1970, pp. 16–22, 72.
10. NT 348264. The current house at Cotehele is mostly Tudor, rebuilt by three generations of the Edgcumbe family in the 15th and 16th centuries with the interior extensively remodelled during the 1650s.
11. Bed: NT 348331. The sketch by W.J. Muller sold in London in 2012. A watercolour (once attributed to William Collingwood) shows a remarkably similar interior view, suggesting the two works may be taken from a third, unknown painting. Thanks to Rachel Hunt, Sarah Medlam and Amanda Bradley for discussion about this.
12. *Cotehele House*, 2005, p. 25.
13. J. Cornforth, 'Cotehele, Cornwall, A property of the National Trust', *Country Life*, 8 February 1990, pp. 68–71; Charles Sandoe Gilbert, *An Historical Survey of the County of Cornwall*, Plymouth, 1817. According to Gilbert, the room owes its name to Charles II, who stayed there before he went into exile. Cornforth went on to write that the embroidery on the bed has been remounted, but the 17th-century knotted fringe is still there.
14. V&A, 517 to 522–1896. 'This embroidery is one of a group of six panels…which came from a house in Hatton Garden, London…The design of the group of panels combines the Baroque style of classical columns, with the exuberant foliage and animal life which is typical of 17th-century English embroidery' [Accessed 15 April 2016: http://collections.vam.ac.uk/item/O77648/wall-hanging-unknown/]. Professional embroiderers produced such hangings as an alternative to more expensive woven tapestries.
15. Many items came from Chatsworth to Burghley in a dowry when Lady Anne Cavendish married John in *c.* 1670. I am grateful to Sheila Landi for this information.
16. Monique King & Donald King, *European Textiles in the Keir Collection, 400BC to 1800AD*, London, 1990, pp. 226, 252.
17. A rare early Turkey-work English carpet, *c.* 1600–30 (NT 130085). We know from photographs that the smaller carpets at Knole were moved about throughout the 19th and 20th centuries.
18. James Lees-Milne, *People and Places: Country House Donors and the National Trust*, London, 1992, chapter 10. Brown wool fabric for these hangings was maintained in recent conservation. See Nicola Gentle, 'Preserving information', Frances Lennard & Patricia Ewer (eds.), *Textile Conservation: Advances in Practice*, Oxford, 2010, pp. 63–69.
19. NT 348153; Nicholas Condy & F.V.J Arundell, *Cotehele on the banks of the Tamar*, 1840.
20. NT 348315.
21. Unpublished report by Simon Jervis for the National Trust, *c.* 2002–03. Assessment of the woodwork is beyond the scope of this article.
22. George Edgcumbe became a fellow of the Society of Antiquaries in 1775. See R. Hunt, *Cotehele*, 2013, p. 22 and Nicola Gentle, 'An Astonishing Survival: The Bed in the Red Room at Cotehele, Cornwall', *Furniture History*, vol. L, 2014, pp. 37–51.
23. Rachel Boak, *Sacred Stitches*, Waddesdon, 2013, p. 14.
24. Information provided by Emma Slocombe.
25. At this date Lady Betty's portrait hung in the adjacent Duchess's Drawing Room.
26. Information provided by Annabel Westman.
27. Emma Slocombe, 'Never all together forgete me', op. cit., pp. 15–17; Emma Slocombe, 'Ancient Furnishing', op. cit., pp. 297–325. A similar quilt made *c.* 1600 is in the V&A (V&A, 616-1886). Embroidered bed covers such as this were made in India for the Portuguese and English market.
28. J.H. Brady, *The Visitor's Guide to Knole*, 1839, pp. 12–13. The early photograph does seem to show at least a double layer of counterpanes.
29. Lionel Sackville-West, *Knole House: its state rooms, pictures and antiquities*, Sevenoaks, 1906, p. 34.
30. J. Cornforth, 'Drayton House, Northamptonshire', *Country Life*, 3 June 1965, pp. 1346–50. Inventories of Drayton House dated 1710 and 1724 include a number of embroidered textiles, particularly collector's items of Indian origin. See Tessa Murdoch (ed.), *Noble households: eighteenth-century inventories of great English houses*, Cambridge, 2006.
31. Noted in an account book of 1886–87 in the Sackville Collection.
32. Bag: NT 130095; embroidered picture: NT 130087.
33. NT 129432. The armchair of *c.* 1700–10 is upholstered in yellow velvet covered up with a loose cover of Jacobean needlework of blue stylised flowers on cream-coloured wool.
34. The upper outer valances, curtains and foot-post sleeves of Lady Betty's bed show evidence of later 20th-century conservation, the current counterpane likewise.

FIG 10 Detail of the canvaswork embroidery on Lady Betty Germain's bed at Knole, Kent
Photo: the author

FIG 11 Detail of the canvaswork embroidery on the King Charles bed at Cotehele, Cornwall
Photo: the author

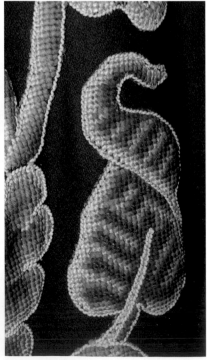